A Heavenly Treatise on the Divine Love of Christ

By John Preston

A Heavenly Treatise on the Divine Love of Christ
By John Preston

Edited and updated by C. Matthew McMahon and Therese B. McMahon
Transcribed by Patti Swearingen

Copyright © 2013 by Puritan Publications and A Puritan's Mind

Some language and grammar has been updated from the original manuscript. Any change in wording or punctuation has not changed the intent or meaning of the original author(s), and has been made to aid the modern reader.

Published by Puritan Publications
A Ministry of A Puritan's Mind
4101 Coral Tree Circle #214
Coconut Creek, FL 33073
www.puritanshop.com
www.apuritansmind.com
www.puritanpublications.com

This Print Edition, 2013
Electronic Edition, 2013
Manufactured in the United States of America

ISBN: 978-1-62663-019-2
eISBN: 978-1-62663-018-5

TABLE OF CONTENTS

MEET JOHN PRESTON

John Preston, D.D. (1587–1628), puritan divine, son of Thomas Preston, a farmer, was born at Upper Heyford in the parish of Bugbrook, Northamptonshire, and was baptized at Bugbrook church on October 27, 1587. His mother's maiden name was Alice Marsh. Her maternal uncle, Creswell, was mayor of Northampton. Being rich and childless, he adopted Preston, placing him at the Northampton grammar school, and subsequently with a Bedfordshire clergyman named Guest for instruction in Greek. He matriculated as a sizar at King's College, Cambridge, on July 5, 1604, his tutor being Busse, who became master of Eton in 1606. King's College was then famous for the study of music; Preston chose "the noblest but hardest instrument, the lute," but made little progress. In 1606 he migrated to Queens' College, where he had as a tutor Oliver Bowles, B.D.

Creswell had left him the reversion of some landed property, and he thought of a diplomatic career. With this view he entered into treaty with a merchant, who arranged for his spending some time in Paris, but on this merchant's death the arrangement fell through. Preston then turned to the study of philosophy, in which he was encouraged by Porter, who succeeded Bowles as his tutor. By Porter's interest with Tyndal, master of Queens and dean of Ely, Preston, who had graduated B.A. in 1607, was chosen fellow in 1609. From philosophy he now turned to medicine; got some practical knowledge under the roof of a friend, a physician in Kent, "very famous for his practice;" and studied astrology, (astrology was then valued as a handmaid to therapeutics).

About 1611, the year in which he commenced to gain an M.A., he heard a sermon at St. Mary's from John Cotton (1585–1652), then fellow of Emmanuel, which opened to him a new career. Cotton had a great reputation as an elegant preacher; but this was a plain evangelical sermon, and "disappointed" his audience.

He returned to his rooms, somewhat mortified by his reception, when Preston knocked at his door, and that close religious friendship began which permanently influenced the lives of both. Preston now gave himself to the study of scholastic divinity; Aquinas seems to have been his favorite; he thoroughly mastered also Duns Scotus and Ockham. The Lord, who designed him to fill an important office in his church, was pleased to frustrate his aspiring thoughts of philsophy. The word of God made so deep an impression on his mind, that at once it cured him of thirsting after preferment. From this time he became remarkable for true christian piety; and though he had here despised the ministerial work as beneath his notice, he now directed all his studies with a view to that sacred employment.

His biographer tells a curious story of his activity in securing the election (1614) of John Davenant as master of Queens in succession to Tyndal. George Montaigne, afterwards archbishop of York, had his eye on this preferment; but immediately on Tyndal's death Preston rode post-haste to London, reaching Whitehall before daybreak. Here he made interest with Robert Carr, Earl of Somerset, with a view to secure court sanction for the choice of Davenant. Returning to

Cambridge, he had the election over before Montaigne got wind of the vacancy.

During the visit of James I to Cambridge in March 1615, Preston distinguished himself as a disputant. He was chosen by Samuel Harsnett, the vice-chancellor, as "answerer" in the philosophy act, but this place was successfully claimed by Matthew Wren (1585–1667), and Preston took the post of "first opponent." His biographer, Thomas Ball, gives an amusing account of the disputation on the question, "Whether dogs could make syllogismes." Preston maintained that they could. James was delighted with his argument (which Granger thinks Preston borrowed from a well-known passage in Montaigne's "Essays"), and introduced a dog story of his own. "It was easy to discerne that ye kings hound had opened a way for Mr. Preston at ye court." Sir Fulke Greville, first lord Brooke, became his firm friend (he ultimately settled 50£ a year upon him). But Preston had by this time given up his early ambition; though he said little of his purpose, his mind was set on the ministry, and he was reading modern divinity, especially Calvin.

His coolness in the direction of court favor gave rise to suspicions of his puritan leaning. These were increased by an incident of James's second visit to Cambridge. A comedy called "Ignoramus," by George Ruggle of Clare Hall, was to be acted before the king. Preston's pupil Morgan (of the Morgans of Heyford), was cast for a woman's part. Preston objected; the lad's guardians overruled the objection; Morgan, who was removed to Oxford, subsequently joined the Roman catholic church. His strictness greatly increased his reputation as a tutor with puritan parents; "he was," says Fuller, "the greatest pulpit-monger in England in man's memory…every time, when Master Preston plucked off his hat to Doctor Davenant, the college master, he gained a chamber or study for one of his pupils." The college buildings were enlarged to provide for the influx of students. He was in the habit of sending those designed for the church to finish their studies with Cotton, now vicar of Boston, Lincolnshire. Meanwhile, Preston's health was suffering, and he was troubled with insomnia. Twice he applied for advice (once in disguise), to William Butler (1535–1618) of Clare Hall, a successful empiric. Butler only told him to take tobacco; on doing so he found his remedy in "this hot copious fume."

Dr. Preston was a divine of extraordinary

abilities and learning, and, about this time, was deeply engaged in public controversy with several learned Arminians. He was called to take a leading part in two public disputations, procured by the Earl of Warwick, and held at York-house, in the presence of the Duke of Buckingham and others of the nobility. The first of these contests was betwixt Bishop Buckridge and Dr. White, dean of Carlisle, on the one part; and Bishop Morton and Dr. Preston, on the other. In the conclusion, the Earl of Pembroke observed, "that no person returned from this learned disputation of Arminian sentiments, who was not an Arminian before he came." The second conference was betwixt Dr. White and Mr. Montague, on the one part; and Bishop Morton and Dr. Preston, on the other. On this occasion, Preston is said to have displayed his uncommon erudition and powers of disputation, to the great advantage of the cause which he undertook to support.

Preston had now taken orders, and become dean and catechist of Queens. He began a course of sermons which were to form a body of divinity. Complaints were made to the vice-chancellor that the college chapel was crowded with scholars from other colleges and townsmen. Order was issued excluding all but members of the college. Preston then began an afternoon lecture at St. Botolph's, of which Queens College is patron. This brought him into conflict with Newcome, commissary to the chancellor of Ely, whose enmity Preston had earned by preventing a match between his pupil, Sir Capel Bedels, and Newcome's daughter Jane. A dispute with Newcome at St. Botolph's delayed the afternoon service; to make room for the sermon, common prayer was for once omitted. Newcome sped to the court at Newmarket to denounce Preston as a nonconformist. The matter came before the heads of houses, and there was talk of Preston's expulsion from the university. At the suggestion of Lancelot Andrewes, then bishop of Ely, Preston was directed to declare his judgment regarding forms of prayer in a sermon at St. Botolph's. He acquitted himself so as to silence complaint. Soon afterwards he was summoned to preach before the king at Finchingbrook, near Royston, Cambridgeshire. James highly approved his argument against the Arminians; he would have shown him less favor had he known that Preston was the author of a paper against the Spanish match, circulated with much secrecy among members of the House of Lords. He was proposed as a royal chaplain by James Hamilton, second marquis of Hamilton, but James thought this premature.

Preston's kinsman, Sir Ralph Freeman, who had married a relative of George Villiers, first duke of Buckingham, now took occasion to represent to Buckingham that he might make friends of the puritans by promoting Preston. Through Buckingham's interest he was made chaplain-in-ordinary to Prince Charles. He took the degree of B.D. in 1620. On Davenant's election (June 11, 1621) to the see of Salisbury, Preston had some expectation of succeeding him as *Margaret professor of divinity*. He felt his Latin to be rusty, and, as an exercise in speaking Latin, he resolved on a visit to the Dutch universities, a project which he carried out with a singular excess of precaution. From the privy council he obtained the necessary license for travel. He said that he was going, the next vacation, to visit Sir Richard Sandys in Kent, and possibly to drink the Tunbridge waters. From the Kentish coast he took a boat for Rotterdam, in a lay habit with "scarlet cloake" and a "gold hat band." In Holland he consorted with Roman Catholics as well as protestants. On his return to Cambridge he met the rumor of his having been beyond the seas with a wonder "at their sillyness, that they would believe so unlikely a relation." After all he had been outwitted, for Williams, the lord keeper, suspecting some puritan plot, had set a spy on his movements, who sent weekly intelligence of his doings.

In February 1622 John Donne (1573–1631) resigned the preachership at Lincoln's Inn, and the benchers elected Preston as his successor. A new chapel, finished soon after his appointment, gave accommodation to the large numbers who flocked to hear him. A more important piece of preferment followed, but it was not obtained without intrigue. Laurence Chaderton, the first master of Emmanuel, had held that post with distinction for thirty-eight years. He had outlived his influential friends, and the fellows thought that to secure Preston's interest with Buckingham would be to the advantage of their college. In particular they wanted a modification of the statutes, which enjoined continuous residence, so cutting them off from chaplaincies and lectureships, and at the same time compelled them to vacate at the standing of D.D., whether otherwise provided or not. From Preston's influence they hoped to gain more liberty, as well as to increase the number of college livings. Chaderton thought highly of Preston, but was very reluctant to resign, and doubted whether, if he did, an Arminian might not be appointed. Preston procured a letter from Buckingham (Sept. 20, 1622) assuring Chaderton that it was the wish of the king and the prince that he should make way for Preston, and promising him a "supply of maintenance." Accordingly Chaderton resigned on Sept. 25; contrary to statute, the vacancy was not announced, on the plea that all the fellows were in residence; the election took place on Oct. 2 with locked gates, and nothing was known of it at Queens until Preston was sent for to be admitted as master of Emmanuel. The statutes limited the master's absence to a month in every quarter. This would interfere with Preston's preaching at Lincoln's Inn. His ingenuity found out evasions to which the fellows consented; the statutes condoned absence in case of "violent detention" and of "college business;" a "moral violence" was held to satisfy the former condition, and a suit at law about a college living, which lasted some years, formed a colourable pretext for alleging college business. But Preston was inflexible on the point of vacating fellowships. In 1623 he was made D.D. by royal mandate. According to Ball, he had been selected by Buckingham to accompany Arthur Chichester, lord

Chichester, on a projected embassy to Germany, and was, on this occasion, made D.D. There is probably some confusion here: Chichester's actual expedition to the palatinate was in May-September 1622.

Preston was anxious for opportunities of preaching at Cambridge, and listened to proposals in 1624 for putting him into a vacant lectureship at Trinity Church. The other candidate, Middlethwait, fellow of Sidney Sussex, was favored by Nicholas Felton, bishop of Ely. The matter was referred to James I, who wanted to keep Preston out of a Cambridge pulpit, and, through Edward Conway (afterwards Viscount Conway), offered him any other preferment at his choice. It was then that Buckingham told Preston he might have the bishopric of Gloucester, vacant by the death of Miles Smith (d. Oct. 20, 1624). But Preston, backed by the townsmen, maintained his ground and got the lectureship.

He was in attendance as Charles's chaplain at Theobalds on Sunday, March 27, 1625, when James I died, and accompanied Charles and Buckingham to Whitehall, where the public proclamation of Charles's accession was made. For the moment it seemed as if Preston was destined to play an important part in politics. He exerted influence on behalf of his puritan friends, obtaining a general preaching license (June 20, 1625) for Arthur Hildersam. But he found his plans counteracted by Laud. On the plea of a danger of the plague, he closed his college and took a journey into the west. He wanted to consult Davenant at Salisbury about the "Appello Cæsarem" of Richard Montagu or Mountague, on which Buckingham had asked his judgment. From Salisbury he went on to Dorchester, and then to Plymouth, where Charles and Buckingham were. When the news reached Plymouth of the disaster at Rochelle (Sept. 16, 1625), Preston did his best to excuse and defend Buckingham against the outburst of protestant indignation. On the removal of Williams from the lord-keepership (Oct. 30, 1625), Buckingham "went so far as to nominate" Preston to be lord keeper. Thomas Coventry, lord Coventry, who had been counsel for Emmanuel College in the suit above mentioned, was eventually appointed.

Preston, however, could not draw the puritans to the side of Buckingham, whom they profoundly distrusted. Preston's friends urged the necessity of a conference on Montagu's books, and nominated on the one side John Buckeridge, bishop of Rochester, and

Francis White, then dean of Carlisle; on the other, Thomas Morton (1564–1659), then bishop of Coventry and Lichfield, and Preston. Buckingham played a double part, begging Preston as his friend to decline the conference, and letting others know what he had done with Preston. The conference was held in February 1626 at York House. Preston refused to take part, but came in after it was begun and sat by as a hearer. A second conference followed in the same month, at which Preston took the lead against Montagu and White.

Buckingham was elected chancellor of Cambridge University on June 1, 1626. Preston did not oppose his election, as Joseph Mead and others did; but he now felt his position in the university insecure, looked to Lincoln's Inn as a refuge in case he were ousted from Cambridge, and as a last resort contemplated a migration to Basle. A private letter to a member of parliament, in which Preston suggested a line of opposition to Buckingham, came by an accident into Buckingham's hands. Seeing that Preston's influence at court was waning, the fellows of Emmanuel petitioned the king to annul the statute limiting the tenure of their fellowships. Buckingham supported their plea. Preston had the support of Sir Henry Mildmay, the founder's grandson. At length a compromise was reached. Charles suspended the statute (May 5, 1627) till such time as six new livings of 100£ a year should be annexed to the college. Buckingham was now engaged with his ill-fated expedition (June 27, 1627) to the Isle of Ré. In November Preston preached before Charles at Whitehall, a sermon which was regarded as prophetic when, on the following Wednesday, news arrived of Buckingham's defeat (Nov.). He was not allowed to preach again, but considered that he had obtained a moral victory for his cause.

Dr. Preston possessed a strong constitution, which he wore out by hard study and constant preaching. His inquiry was not, "How long have I lived?" but, "how have I lived?" Desiring, in his last sickness, to die among his old friends, he retired to Preston, near Heyford, in his native county; and having revised his will, and settled all his worldly affairs, he committed himself to the wise and gracious disposal of his heavenly Father. As he felt the symptoms of death coming upon him, he said, "I shall not change my company; for I shall still converse with God and saints."

A few hours previous to his departure, being told it was the Lord's day, he said, "A fit day to be sacrificed on! I have accompanied saints on earth: now I shall accompany angels in heaven. My dissolution is at hand. Let me go to my home, and to Jesus Christ, who hath bought me with his precious blood." He afterwards added, "I feel death coming to my heart. My pain shall now be turned into joy," and then gave up the ghost, in the month of July, 1628, being only forty-one years of age. His remains were interred in Fausley church, when the venerable Mr. Dod preached his funeral sermon to an immense crowd of people. Fuller, who has classed him among the learned writers of Queen's college, Cambridge, says, " he was all judgment and gravity, and the perfect master of his passions, an excellent preacher, a celebrated disputant, and a perfect politician."

A fine engraved portrait of him is prefixed to his "New Covenant," 1629; it is poorly reproduced in Clarke; there are also two smaller engravings. As Ball describes him, "he was of an able, firme, well-tempered constitution, comely visadge, vigorous and vived eye." He was unmarried. His will provided for his mother and brothers, founded exhibitions at Emmanuel College, and left his books and furniture to Thomas Ball, his favorite pupil and his minute biographer.

Preston's early inclination for diplomacy was symptomatic of his character, which Fuller has summed as that of "a perfect politician," apt "to flutter most on that place which was furthest from his eggs." He had great self-command, kept his own counsel, and was impervious to outside criticism. Only to Ball does he seem to have frankly bared his mind, and Ball's admiring delineation of him furnishes a singular picture of cautious astuteness and constitutional reserve. It is clear that his heart was firmly set on the propagation of Calvinistic theology; his posthumous works (edited by Richard Sibbes, John Davenport, Thomas Ball, and partly by Thomas Goodwin, D.D.) are a storehouse of argument in its favor.

His works are:

1. "The Saints Daily Exercise; or a ... Treatise of Prayer," *etc.*, 3rd edit. 1629, 4to (on 1 Thess. v. 17). 2. "The New Covenant" ... 14 Sermons on Genesis, 17:1, 2, *etc.*, 1629, 4to. 3. "Four Sermons," *etc.*, 1630, 4to (on Eccles. 9:1, 2, 11, 12). 4. "Five Sermons ... before his Majestie," *etc.*, 1630, 4to (on 1 John 5:15; Isaiah, 64:4; Eph. 5:15; 1 Tim. 3:15; 1

Sam. 12:20–22). 5. "The Breastplate of Faith and Love," *etc.* 1630, 4to (eighteen sermons, on Rev. 1:17; 1 Thess. 1:3; Gal. 5:6). 6. "The Doctrine of the Saints Infirmities," *etc.*, Amsterdam [1630?], 12mo (on 2 Chron. 20:18–20). 7. "Life Eternal; or a...Treatise...of the Divine...Attributes in 17 Sermons," *etc.* 1631, 4to. 8. "The Law Out Lawed," *etc.* Edinburgh, 1631, 4to (on Rom. vi. 14). 9. "An Elegant ... Description of Spiritual Life and Death," *etc.*, 1632, 4to. 10. "The Deformed Form of a Formal Profession," *etc.*, Edinburgh, 1632, 4to (on 2 Tim. 3:5); London, 1641, 4to. 11. "Sins Overthrow; or a...Treatise of Mortification," *etc.*, 2nd edit. 1633, 4to (on Col. 3:5). 12. "Four...Treatises," *etc.* 1633, 4to (includes 1. "A Remedy against Covetousnes," on Col. 3:5; 2. "An Elegant and Lively Description of Spiritual Life and Death," on John 5:25; 3. "The Doctrine of Self-denial," on Luke 9:23, preached at Lincoln's Inn; 4. "Three Sermons upon the Sacrament," on 1 John 5:14). 13. "The Saints Qualification," *etc.*, 3rd edit. 1634, 4to (ten sermons on Humiliation, nine of them on Rom. 1:18, the tenth preached before the House of Commons on Num. 25:10, 11; nine sermons on Sanctification, on 1 Cor. 5:17; three on communion with Christ in the Sacrament, on 1 Cor. 10:16). 14. "A Liveles Life; or Man's Spiritual Death," *etc.*, 3rd edit. 1635, 4to (on Eph. 2:1–3). 15. "A Sermon preached at Lincolnes-Inne," *etc.*, 1635, 4to (on Gen. 22:14). 16. "Remains of ... John Preston," 2nd edit. 1637, 4to (includes 1. "Judas his Repentance," on Matt. 27:3–5; 2. "The Saints Spiritual Strength," on Eph. 3:16; 3. "Paul's Conversion," on Acts 9:6). 17. "The Golden Scepter...Three Treatises," *etc.*, 1638, 4to. 18. "Mount Ebal...Treatise of the Divine Love," *etc.*, 1638, 4to (five sermons on 1 Cor. 16:22). 19. "The Saints Submission," *etc.*, 1638, 12mo. 20. "The Fullness of Christ," *etc.*, 1640, 4to (on John 1:16). 21. "The Christian Freedom," *etc.* 1641, 4to (on Rom. 6:14). 22. "De Irresistibilitate Gratiæ Convertentis. Thesis habita in Scholis Publicis Academiæ Cantabrigiensis ... Ex ipsius manuscripto," *etc.* 1643, 16mo; in English, "The Position of John Preston...Concerning the Irresistiblenesse of Converting Grace," *etc.* 1654, 4to. 23. "Riches of Mercy," *etc.*, 1658, 4to. 24. "Prayers," *etc.*, 24mo; this last is in the list of works prefixed to "The Position." An "Abridgment" of six of Preston's works by William Jemmat was published in 1648, 12mo. With his sermons are sometimes erroneously catalogued some funeral sermons (1615–19) by John Preston, vicar of East Ogwell, Devonshire.

(Taken in part from the National Dictionary of biography,

Oxford, 1896)

Sources include:

The *Life of Preston*, by Thomas Ball, written in 1628, several times printed in an abridged form by Samuel Clarke, the martyrologist (whose last edition is in his Lives of Thirty-two English Divines, 1677, pp. 75 sq.), is full and graphic; the chronological arrangement is sometimes confused (see also Clarke's *Life of John Cotton* in the same collection, p. 219); it was edited in 1885 by E. W. Harcourt, esq., from the original manuscript at Nuneham. Fuller's *Church History*, 1655, xi. 119, 126, 131; Fuller's *Worthies*, 1662 (Northamptonshire), p. 291; Burnet's History of his Own Time, 1724, i. 19; Granger's *Biographical Hist. of England*, 1779, ii. 174, sq.; Middleton's *Biographia Evangelica*, 1780, ii. 406 sq.; Brook's *Lives of the Puritans*, 1813, ii. 356 sq.; Neal's *Hist. of the Puritans* (Toulmin), 1822, ii. 124 sq.; Heywood and Wright's *Cambridge University Transactions*, 1854, ii. 312 sq.; extracts from the *University Register, Cambridge*, per the master of Emmanuel, and from the burial register at Fawsley, per the Rev. P. W. Story.

ORIGINAL TITLE PAGE

A HEAVENLY TREATISE
on the
Divine Love of
CHRIST

Showing,
1. The Motives thereof
2. The Means thereof
3. The Marks thereof
4. The Kinds thereof

Delivered in five sermons by
JOHN PRESTON, DOCTOR IN DIVINITY,
Chaplain in ordinary to his Majesty, Master of
Emmanuel College in Cambridge, and sometimes
Preacher at Lincolnes Inn.

Matthew 22:37-38
"This is the first and great commandment: thou shalt
love the Lord thy God with all thy heart."

LONDON
Printed by *Thomas Paine*, for *John Stafford*, in Chancery
Lane, overagainst the Roules.
1640

TO THE READER

To the Reader of these pious and plain sermons, *Grace and Peace.*

Christian Reader, it was an old complaint of a heathen that the noise of the old philosophers opinions hindered their *dunghill gods* from hearing their prayers. And it is not a very new complaint of a Christian, that the many idle subtleties of the school have so drawn up Divinity to the highest peg of a curious mind, that it hinders the heart from molding it into prayers and practice.

This grave and serious Divine, whose living sermons are here commended to you when he is dead, saw it with both eyes. Therefore, though he was no small master in subtleties, yet all his thoughts were bent to draw them down from the floating brain, to the feeling heart, that his hearer might be better brought to know and do. As this has been his course in all his writings before published, so is it in this, that now comes to your hands. How might he have hid himself in the thorns of speculation? How high might he have flown in the curious extracts of every word of this text?

But he that delighted to speak ten words to edification, rather than ten thousand that could not pierce every ordinary brain, contented himself to fill up deep wells to make them drinkable and to wade the sweet and shallow streams of the love of the Lord Jesus.

He might, from here, have set himself up on the mount of cursings, and showered down worse than fire and brimstone on delinquents, but the meekness of his spirit carries him up to the mount of blessings, to teach good souls through death, to find life through threatenings to meet with comforts.

He, being lifted up by the divine love of Christ, describes love, and our love to Christ. He soars to the equity and necessity of it. He does not rest before he has given you the means, motives, marks, gains, qualification, and objects of this love. How he would have you effectually love the Lord Jesus, that you may avoid the curse and enjoy the blessings. He knew nothing more necessary for a good Christian then this love. First, he must be a Christian by faith. Next, he must live as a Christian by faith and love *too*. He can do neither without the love of Christ to him, and this he cannot have but in his time. He shall have faith in Christ, and love to the Lord Jesus.

There is neither thing nor love in the entire world more comfortable to a good man than this. Sin presses down hard and pulls him back from heaven. Satan baits both the hands, and hooks of the world, prosperity, and adversity to entangle him. Death brings him down to the bed of darkness, the land of oblivion, and lays him up as a despised lump. But if he has this love when all vanishing bubbles fly away, this mounts him up into the bosom of God. As water, be it conveyed in pipes never so low, yet in the same pipes it will rise up as high as the spring head. So this love springing from the bosom of God though it is shed abroad, and runs through the channels of our hearts on earth, yet with a willing motion it mounts up to Christ again, and carries us along with it despite of storms. Where we love, we live. Where we love, we desire to be, and God has so ordered that this appetite shall not be in vain.

And as for other loves, see whether the love of the Lord Jesus does not surpass them all. Love other things and yet often they slide away from you, so that in them you have but a momentary joy. But love your Lord, and doing so, he abides with you forever, and is to you a spring of everlasting joy. Love other things and they cannot know the sincerity of your heart, how much, and in what manner and measure you love them. But love your Lord, and he knows better the love of your heart then yourself. You may say unto him, as did Peter: *You know all things, you know that I love you,* and shall find entertainment answerable. Love other things and you have vexing care over them, both about their gaining, keeping and losing. But love your Lord and your care is sweet for him, yes he cares for you in all your ways. You can lose nothing by it. No, not your heart, which though it goes out to him, and he keeps it, yet he gives it to you again, and that is better than it was to comfort you in your whole course.

Love other things and you find them not at all times nor so often as you would, when you have need, you cannot speak to them so often as you would, neither do they harken to your words as you could. But love your Lord and he is with you always to the end of the world. You may speak to him at any time by night or by day. He hears you at all times, and gives you your hearts desires. Love other things, and you cannot know their secrets. There may be something in them which may be vexations to you in this matter. There may be a snake under the green grass, a filthy goad under a sweet flower, and a worm in the heart of a desired apple. But love your Lord, and he will reveal the mystery of godliness and his hidden secrets of truth unto you according to his word, Yes, you shall see that nothing but that which is glorious in itself, and good for you is either in him, or about him.

Love other things, and they put you to many a trouble. They hinder you in your prayers, and all your service to God, because you do always think and dote upon them. But love your lord, and he brings into your heart and conscience, peace which passes all understanding. The more you love him when you pray, the more he gives you to yourself. Yes, the more he gives you to himself and fills you with holy comfort. Love other things, and they are without you still. You can never bring them to any more intimate communion, save that which is common to you with Epicurus. But love the Lord, and he dwells *in you,* and *you in him,* for he is love.

Love other things, and they seek at your hands a profit and gain to themselves, or else they perish in your love. They will take advantage of your love to work on you for their own perfections. But love your Lord, and he seeks your profit and protection. He always endures to glorify himself in doing you good.

Love other things, and most times they will deceive you. They are often liars, variable, and inconstant. But love your Lord, and you shall be assured, he is most true and unchangeable, and you must build on him, that he will not fail you nor forsake you.

Love other things and oftentimes they cause grief and heaviness, and so do highly displease you. But love your Lord, and it banishes fear and sad confusion of face because you cannot see anything in him that can displease you. Lastly, love other things and you know not assuredly whether you are to ever love of them again. But love your Lord, and you may be assured that he answers you with the same. Yes, with a better answer, for he cannot but love a blessed child of the begetting of his own will.

By how much more excellent this love is then the love of all things else, by so much the more must you press to enjoy and practice it. Everything naturally desires that which is best for it. If it does not have it, it is from the error about the object, or the miscarriage of the appetite. That therefore you may fail in neither, but may have the best object, and the best appetite cleared from clouds of ignorance and sin to you.

These five sermons of an experienced master in

Israel are tendered to you. If you reap benefit by them, give glory to God who would not have this lamp of love kept under a bushel and buried in oblivion.

If you receive the least encouragement from these foregoing lines to make use of this light, know that they proceed from the love of you in Christ, in him, who desires your prayers, that he may love the Lord Jesus both in life and death.

Farewell.

A HEAVENLY TREATISE ON
THE DIVINE LOVE OF CHRIST
SERMON 1

1 Cor. 16:22 "If any man love not the Lord Jesus Christ, let him be *anathema, maranatha.* (Let him be had in execration or let him be excommunicated unto the death.)"

These words have little dependence on the words going before this which are these; *the salutation of me, Paul, with my own hands.* It was the custom of the Apostle, that the church might not be deceived with counterfeit Epistles to set his name to those he wrote. And that he would not go along, but did always add some gracious sentence as commonly this: *The grace of our Lord Jesus Christ be with you all.* And there he adds that sentence which so suits with the spirit and mind of St. Paul, that it might easily show it to be St. Paul's Epistle, a man so abounding in the love of the Lord, as he is zealous against such as do not love him. We shall find in all St. Paul's preaching that faith and love were that which he drove at, those two roots, those two pillars on which the church is built from where all the rest flow. By this, he is teaching ministers what they should beat at, what should be their aim. And so people are taught here what to do. They must water these two roots well, and then the branches will flourish. Our wisdom should be to look to these, for these being strong, all will be strong. If these are weak, all will be weak. *If any man does not love the Lord Jesus, let him be had in execration, yes, accursed unto the death.* His scope is to commend love to the *Corinthians.* It is as if Paul would say, If I should cast about me to commend some special thing to you now at the closing up of my Epistle, I know nothing better than this *Love of the Lord Jesus.* And there are two reasons why you should love him. First, you are in a miserable and accursed condition if you do not do it. And the second is from the object you are to love, he is the Lord and so many will challenge your love, *Jesus your Savior,* and so has well deserved it so that we have here an exhortation and two reasons of it. The words have little difficulty. Something I will say of the two words in the original *Anathema* and *Maranatha.* The word *Anathema* signifies the separation of a thing to *destruction. Maranatha* is a Syrian word, signifying *cursing,* taken from the Hebrew root, and signifies more than

Anathema. The Apostle doubles this curse to show the greatness of the punishment. It is a great punishment which he would express in two languages. The general doctrine we will observe from these words is this; DOCTRINE: *That to love the Lord Jesus is so necessarily required of us, that he is worthy to be cursed that do not do it.*

Doctrine 1. Sometimes in Scripture the promise is made to faith, sometimes to repentance, and sometimes to love. Love is so required that without it, a man is worthy to be accursed, yes, and shall be cursed. I will but open and apply this, not standing to prove it. And first, I will show what love is in general. Secondly, what this love of the Lord Jesus is, to show how it works. And thirdly, how they come to be worthy to be accursed, that do not love him. And first, love is among the affections which are planted in the *will*, and it may be described this way: *It is a disposition of the will and heart of man, by which it turns and inclines to some good, which it apprehends to be agreeable to its own nature.* This is what love is in general. The will is carried to nothing but that which is apprehended to be good. Now this love is a principle act of the will, and it must be an agreeable good to him whose will inclines to it. An envious man may confess the excellencies of another man, but he hates them, he suffers by them. They seem not to be an agreeable good to him. And this may be illustrated by the contrary. Hate is that by which a man turns from a thing which he apprehends contrary to himself. This love shows itself in two effects; first, it desires the preservation of what it loves, that it may be kept safe. *How love shows itself.* Secondly, it desires union with it, that they may draw nearer to one another; that which you desire may be yours, with which you desire conjunction. Now sometimes a thing may be nearer, sometimes too far off, therefore it desires such a nearness as may stand with its convenience. And this is common to all love. If you love a glass, you will take care that it is kept clean and whole, and for your use. So, if you love a horse, you will take care that he is well and in a good case, and that he is yours. We see the same in the love of a Father to his Son, of one friend to another. This is the nature of love.

Now hate contrariwise desires the destruction of that which is hated, that it may be taken out of the world, and if that cannot be, it desires separation from it, as far as it is. And so you have seen the nature of love in general.

Now there are divers kinds of love. There is a

love of pity when you desire the preservation of a man's person, and the removing of some ill quality. As, our Savior mourned in Spirit, for the hardness of their hearts. He pitied them, and yet was angry with their sin.

The kinds of love. There is a *love of desire,* when a thing is desired to be kept safe for our use. And this is for the inferior faculties, as sight loves a pleasant object and so it should be continued to be seen.

There is a *love of complacence,* when we look on a thing, in which all the faculties are pleased, not only the inferior, but the superior as the mind and the will.

There is a *love of friendship* when a man loves where he is loved again, when love is reciprocal, there is an intercourse of love.

There is a *love of dependence* when we love him on whom we depend, and so we love God when we look on him as on whom all our good depends, so that we love him more than ourselves because our good depends on him, more than on ourselves.

The qualities of love. We will add the qualities of love. There is *a natural love* planted in us by nature as the parents to their children, of one man to other. This love is indifferent, not good in itself, good not otherwise than directed on a good object.

There is a *sinful love*, arising from sinful habits which seek things convenient to it; as nothing is better than love on a right object for there is nothing worse than love on a wrong object. As natural love puts us in the condition of normal men, so this sinful love makes men worse than beasts, and equals them with the Devil.

There is a *spiritual love* arising out of holy qualities which seeks an object agreeable to it. And this makes a man above a man, and in some sort equal with the angels. Man are as they love. God judges us by our affections. We are judge by what we love. He that loves wickedness is truly a wicked man. He that loves holiness is truly holy. This foundation that we have laid, though it may seem somewhat remote, yet you shall find it of use to hold up this building before we are done with the point. (cf. Isa 9, 2 Cor. 1:20, 1 Cor 5.)

What this love of the Lord Jesus is. The second thing that we have to declare is what this love of the Lord Jesus is. Now the best way to show what this is, is to show how it is worked. Now, for its working there must be two antecedent things which must make way for it, and they are *humiliation* and *faith*. For everyone does not believe this to be needful and if they do believe it, yet they may be opposed to it because it is not agreeable to their nature. That a man must be broken so, and molded again, before he can have this love which is worked by humiliation and faith. And they are wrought on your soul when we preach the gospel and *offer Jesus Christ* in it. For the duty of a minister is nothing but this, to *offer Jesus Christ* himself to the world. "For unto us a child is born, to us a son is given, for unto you is born a Savior, that is, Christ the Lord." This is the summary of the gospel. This is the news which we bring. God has given us his son. We do not offer you forgiveness of sin, but the *Lord Jesus*. And when he has *given us him, will he not with him give us all things also?* Christ must first be given, and when you have him, you shall have all, for in him are the promises, *yes* and *Amen*. First have Christ, and then the promises belong to you, but not before. The gospel shows us that God the Father is willing to give you his Son. Ministers are his spokesmen, to beseech you to take him, that you would take him as your husband, to be *ruled* by him. None, before you, no matter how humble, can marry you to Christ. You must be divorced from all other things, and believe that Christ will take you, and this is *faith*, and it is done in humiliation. And then when you can receive him you will love him.

Now when we preach this to the world, what answer do we find? Why, there are some that will not believe that there is such a Lord, and then our work is to persuade that Christ is the Lord and this was the Apostles work and theirs at the beginning. But when we entreat you to take Christ for your Lord, your answer is as theirs who were invited to the feast. This and that excuse they have to hinder them to believe that a Christ is propounded and men do not regard him; they will not look after him. Now, that Christ may be received there is required humiliation and faith. Humiliation opens their eyes, by the Law, and spirit of bondage, that they see themselves miserable men, men condemned to die. Now when God has discovered our misery to us, and we rightly apprehend what our estate is, then we begin to look on Christ as a condemned malefactor on his pardon, as a captain on him that comes to redeem him, as a widow that thought she should live well enough alone, but now when all her goods as seized upon, and they are not to carry her to prison, would be content if no one would marry her. When a man shall see what he is without Christ, one that is condemned that must perish if he does not have him, then he looks on Christ as on one most desirable to prize him, to thirst for him, and if he knows that Christ will then receive him, O then he cannot but love him. For love (as has been said) is to a good notion apprehended, and fit for us. Now without this, we will think of Christ, as if we might be well enough without him. But when the heart is in this way prepared by humiliation, O that all the world would vanish for Christ. Then the gospel comes and tells us that Christ is willing to take us, to redeem us, to be ours. And then when we take him, the match is made up and there arises this conjugal love. The Apostle prays for the Ephesians, "that Christ may dwell in their hearts by faith," Eph. 3, to unite them to Christ, to marry him, then presently it follows, *that you may be rooted and grounded in love.* So that love follows this, and not a flash, but it roots us in love. The act of justifying faith, is the taking of Christ for rest. Now when you have taken him thus, then you will love him and then all that follows will be effects of this love, so that this love of the Lord Jesus is this; in other words: *A holy disposition arising from faith, by which we cleave to the Lord Jesus Christ with full purpose of heart, to serve and please him in all things.*

By which we cleave to him. Love inclines and knits our hearts to him, as it did David's to Jonathan's. And so Barnabas exhorted them to *cleave unto the Lord with full purpose of heart*, (Acts 11). Neither is this idle, but makes a man desirous to please the Lord in all things. A man is said to love the Lord when out of a persuasion that Christ is most desirable and willing to receive him, he cleaves to the Lord with a desire to serve and please him in all things. Faith that begets love is not only a persuasion that the Lord will be merciful and forgive us. (For a prisoner may see the judge willing to pardon him, and persuade himself that he shall be pardoned, and yet not love the judge because he does not look on the judge, as on an amiable person, but a receiving and resting upon us as amiable. There is another affection when the heart is so framed, it apprehends Christ for its only good, and its happiness. Faith is not only an act of the mind to believe that God will pardon us, but of the will and heart also, to take Christ for our husband, so that all the parts of the heart are inclined and bent after him. *If you believe with all your heart*, says *Philip* to the Eunuch, (Acts 8). If a spouse should see one willing to have her, that is not enough to make up the match, she may not think him fit, she may be unwilling. But suppose there is one that she loves above all, whom she thinks to be most fit for her, yes she thinks she shall be undone if she does not have him, but yet she is not sure that he will have her, but thinks it is very probable that he may be induced to it. So this is faith when a man sees Christ only worth his love, he would gladly be divorced from all, so that he might have Christ, O he cannot be without him, yet there is something betwixt them, he cannot firmly believe that Christ loves him, but yet does not think that he is wholly averse from him. Though your persuasion is not full, yet if you have this thirst and desire, this hungering after Christ, you may be comforted. This shuts out such as have a persuasion of the pardon of their sins, and yet do not have this love, this prizing, this desiring after Christ, and takes in those things that love and prize him, yet do not find that full persuasion of his love, so, that this love is that which follows humiliation and faith, the breaking of the heart and the molding of it up again. When we see our need of him, and his willingness to receive us, then we will take him that cannot be without this love to him.

Why they are worthy to be cursed that do not love the Lord Jesus. Now we come to the third thing, the reason why they are worthy to be accursed to the death that do not love the Lord Jesus. This may seem strange and harsh. What then comes of all unregenerate men? The Apostle means that such as continue in their not loving the Lord or such as have sinned against the Holy Spirit. But the former sense I take to be the best, neither is this any strange thing, for it is one part of the gospel. There are two parts of the gospel: *If you believe, you shall be saved, if you do not believe, you shall be damned.* Sometimes it is if you repent you shall be saved, or if you do not, you shall perish. So, if you love you shall be saved. If you do not love, you shall be accursed. Now why should he pitch on such a frame of words to express their condition?

Reason. Because when Christ shall come and be a suitor to us, when he shall *woo* us, and offer himself to us, and we will have none of him, then the Son becomes angry, (Psalm 2). When he shall offer himself to us, and none will kiss him, then he becomes *angry to death*, and they perish in the way. Those whom do not love him, his love turns to anger and the greatest hatred. So, when the Father sent to call them to the feast that were invited, and they refused it, this made him wrathful, (Matt. 11). When we shall come to preach Christ to men, when this light hid from the beginning of the world shall shine, and you shall despise it and condemn it, know that now is the ax laid to the root of the tree.

God will bear it at your hands no longer. Now if a man will not love the Lord Jesus, let him be had in execration, yes, let him be accursed to the death.

If a man does not keep the Law, he is to be cursed. Now there was a double keeping of the law. A *legal* keeping which answers the exact rigor of the law, an *evangelical keeping* which is an earnest endeavoring to keep the law, and to make a man's heart as perfect as may be. Now there being more mercy in this, there is a greater curse on its breach. Now love is the fulfilling of the law, and not to love the Lord is not to keep the law, and therefore the curse follows it.

If a man does not love the Lord Jesus, it is because he loves something better than him. It may be you love your wealth more than Christ. And are you not worthy to be cursed for it? It may be you are lovers of pleasure more than of God, and does not this deserve a curse? It may be you love the praise of men before that of God, and is not this to be accursed? Adultery was punished with death, and what punishment then is enough for the going a whoring from such a God after such vanities?

Again, cursing belongs to hypocrites. "Woe be unto you Scribes and Pharisees, hypocrites," (Matt 23).

Now what a man does not out of love is done out of hypocrisy, which is to do the outward action without the inward affection as counterfeit gold has the same stamp and color with true gold. But, as we cast away counterfeit silver and gold, set it apart to destruction, nailing them up that they may be known. So will God deal with such as serve him outwardly without this love to him?

Love is that which commands all in a man. It is as the rudder to a ship; all follows love. When a man does not love the Lord, everything goes from him. Now when the whole man shall go from the Lord, is not such a one worthy to be cursed, yes to be had in execration to death?

The point behind verse 1. It is a great sin not to love the Lord Jesus. If this love of the Lord is so necessary, then see what a sin it is, when an execrable thing it is, not to love the Lord, and what you are to think of yourselves if you do not love the Lord. When Jesus Christ shall be propounded to men, and this light is great, but men do resist it and do not embrace the Lord. When we see this, we should have such a spirit as Paul, (for this was out of the abundance of his zeal), we should, I say, be stirred against such with a holy indignation, (cf. Acts

17). "Do not I hate those that hate thee?" Psalm 139. Yes, I hate them with a perfect hatred. "This you have that you hate the works of Nicholaitans which thing also I hate." Rev. 8:2 and this was a sign of Lot's sincerity that his righteous soul was grieved, and *vexed with the unclean conversation of the Sodomites*, 2 Peter 2. If you can see Christ scorned and rejected, and his Word slighted, and his *blood trampled* on, and you yourselves are not moved with it, you are not of Paul's spirit, who speaking of some *whose God was their belly, whose glory was their shame, of whom (he says) I have told you often and now tell you weeping, that they are the enemies of the cross of Christ*, Phil. 3. Where did this come from, but out of the abundance of his love to Christ, and mankind? I wish you would all look to yourselves whether you are in this number or not, of those that do not love the Lord. This is such a sin, as the curse is doubled on it, and the punishment is but to show the measure of the sin. He does not thunder out of his curse against him that opposes the Lord, or resists him, but against him that does not love the Lord. The Apostle, as *Moses*, gets him up to *Mount Ebal*, and whom did he curse? Even all such as do not love the Lord Jesus. This doctrine thoroughly considered may let in a crevice of light to you that now you may look on yourself as on a execrable thing which God hates, and you must see God, even stretching out his power to confound you, yes, you may see the *gospel* cursing you.

Objection. But what terror is there in the preaching of the gospel, you will say?

Solution. O much more (my brethren) than may be expressed, for the curse of the Law was not so preemptory, though we have plain words for, yet it was not without all condition. But God swears to this curse as if we were thus cursed if we would continue to love him. The law is the proper instrument of humbling, yet the gospel humbles more for sin is the matter of humiliation. And there is sins against the gospel, yet greater sins than against the law when you hear the curse of the law. "Cursed be he that continues not in everything that is written in the book of the Law, to do them," (Galatians 3). You will say you will go to Christ and he shall do it for you, but when the gospel curses such as do not love Christ, to whom will you go to love God? Another man cannot love for you, and if you think this to be too harsh, let this verse sound often in your ears.

If any man does not love the Lord Jesus Christ, let him be accursed unto the death.

This cannot be altered. It is the Word of God. Ask then yourself this question, whether you love the Lord, or no? And do not put yourself off with your hope, but try your love, for love will have sensible strings in the heart, it will drive you close to the Lord to keep in with him, to have communion with him.

Signs of love. Do you then feel that you are never well but when you are with him, and yet do you not love him? Do you walk with God as Enoch did? Will any of you say that a wife loves her husband which for her good will never be with him?

Love is also very diligent and laborious. You will never leave until you get near him whom you love. No labor will be tedious to get his favor. Many years seem a few days to Jacob to serve for Rachel because he loved her.

Again, love is not of a deferring nature, but is impatient of all delays.

Again, love is content with itself. It does not need to be hired to love, *Amor est sibi ipsi dulce pabulum.* It carries its meat in its own mouth. If you love the Lord Jesus, you would not ask what wages you should have to love him.

Again, love is a strong impulsive quality. It carries you on impetuously to the Lord. It is a fire that breaks through thick and thin so that he that loves cannot sin willfully if he would, he cannot but obey, he cannot do anything against the gospel. He must do all things for it. *The love of Christ constrains me, says St. Paul, 2 Corinthians 5.* Look how a man is carried with a strong stream or by a strong man whom he cannot resist. So his love compelled him. I preach, and preach, and men think me mad, but I cannot but do it. The love of Christ constrains me, and as it constrains me, so there is nothing more different than constraint and not to do it. The effects of this law are so violent as if they were compelled, but for the manner of working, nothing is so contrary to it as compulsion, for you love him and we are carried to it, as a stone to the center. You would do no otherwise.

So ends the first Sermon.

SERMON 2

Matt. 22:37-38, "This is the first and great commandment: thou shalt love the Lord thy God with all they heart."

Psalm 31:26, "Love the Lord O all ye his saints."

1 Cor. 16:22, "If any man love not the Lord Jesus Christ, let him be had in execration, yes let him be accursed unto the death."

Point of Application. Verse 2. Try whether what you do is out of love. That love to the Lord Jesus is so necessarily required that he is worthy to be accursed that does not have it. Then here you are to consider your condition, and to examine yourself. It may be this is your condition and it may be a thing you never considered, or at least, you never knew the danger of it. Therefore, now see what you case is. The best service we can do to you is to show you your estates, if you are right, to comfort you, and if you are not right, is it not best for you to know while it may be amended? You that live in the church and have gone far, examine yourself in this.

Have you done all out of love? You have kept yourself in good course. You keep the Lord's Day and live like a Christian. You do many things indeed, but let me ask you this question. Do you do all of this out of love? For without love all is nothing. If a man should be a martyr, (which is the highest action), yet without this love, it is to no purpose, *1 Corinthians 13*. Put the case before you, a man should do many things for you, yet if he does not do it out of love to you, you cannot regard it. *Neither circumcision, nor uncircumcision avails anything but faith which works by love, Galatians 5*. It is all one whether you pray or not, hear or not, live well or not, if it is not out of love. What was said of circumcision or uncircumcision may be said of any duty, all that you have done is as nothing if it is not out of love. Try yourselves by this, for I do not know in all the frames of theology, such a touchstone of hypocrisy as this. This most unmasks a man of anything. As it was with the Apostle, *the law revived and he died, Romans 7.* So, it may be you have thought yourself a living man, see then if you love. Do not deceive yourself any longer.

This is a doctrine of much importance if God would convey it with majesty by the power of his Spirit. It would amaze and startle the stoutest stomach to hear, *Cursed is he that does not love the Lord.* If you love the Lord, he will bear much with you. See what a testimony he gives of David for all his failings. But do what you will for him without love, and he will regard it but as a complement. As man counts that a complement not to be regarded with which the heart does not go, so does God. Look to it, therefore, that you love the Lord Jesus, for it is a thing of great consequence, for the curse follows you if you do not.

You are now therefore to examine yourself, whether you love or not. And to help you in it, I will lay down some marks of this love, but first set down with yourself this conclusion, *If I do not love the Lord Jesus, I am an accursed man.*

Another Point of Application. There are some notes to make in order to try this love to the Lord Christ. Do you feel this love in you? Have you a sense of it? Ammon was sick of love so that his friends could see him wear away. To the spouse, Solomon says *I am sick of love*, Song of Songs 2. And do you love the Lord and cannot feel it? Do you feel your heart working towards God? This love is a thing that one would think needs no marks, you cannot but see it. It is noted in love, so, that if you did love the Lord, you would have a longing desire after him. There will be joy in the fruition of him, anger against all impediments to it; grief when he withdraws himself, hope when there is any probability of enjoying him, fear to lose him. Now do not deceive yourself, you who love the Lord, you will say, but is this love *to his person, or to his kingdom, his goods*? When you present Jesus Christ alone to yourself, can you then love him? *The virgins love him, the harlots love him.* And there is a great deal of harlotry love in the world, to the Lord Jesus. It was one thing to love Alexander, another to love the King. It is true, Christ is a great King that can do much good or evil in the world, and so many may love him. But can you answer this question, "Loveth thou me?" With Peter, "Yea, Lord; thou knowest that I love thee. (John 21:16). You that know my heart and the secret turnings of it, can bear me witness that I love you.

Do you love his company? Love is seen in nothing more than this. Do you love his presence, to walk with God? Do you observe all his dealings to you from morning to night, refer all still unto him? Are you still in dealings with him? Still you have something to do with him, there is not an hour that passes you in which you do not have recourse to him. When Christ takes a man to himself, *I will come in to him, and will sup with him, and he with me,* (Rev. 3:20). Do you have, then, this communion with Christ? Does he sup with you, dwell with you? Now, communion stands in speaking to another, and in hearing him speak to us. When you pray, do you pray formally as one that is glad when the duty is over? O! if you loved the Lord, you would never be better than when you are at prayer. And you would go to prayer as you would go to speak with your dearest friend. So do you hunger after the Word which is the character of Christ, his will, his love-letter? Put the case to thought, a woman should have her husband at the East Indies, how welcome would a letter be to her from him? Therefore, Moses that loved God, desired to see his glory, Exodus 33, to know him better, to grow more acquainted with him. Now what the word does to you, it shows to you that glory which Moses saw.

If you love the Lord, holy days and sacrament days would be as feast days and wedding days, for then you meet with God more nearly. Do you then put off your coming to the Sacrament, and would you not come near it for the speech of some, and yet will you say that you love the Lord? Where love is, there is delight. A man delights in his fellowship whom he loves, whom you have not seen, yet you love him. Yes, whom though you do not see him, yet you believe and speak with joy *unspeakable* and *glorious*. Do you then delight in his presence? For delight will be in the enjoying of that which we love. Joy follows love.

To delight in a man's company is that mark of love which cannot be dissembled. Do you then, *love God, and into the patient waiting for Christ*, (2 Thess. 3:5). If one should bring you news that you must go to the Lord, or he would come to you tomorrow, would this be acceptable news to you? Does he bring good tidings? If a spouse should have her betrothed husband beyond the seas, and should hear of his return, if she should say that it were the worst news that could come to her, would you think that she loved him? No, there could not come a more welcome messenger to you than such a one if you did love the Lord. Blessed are the dead that die in the Lord (for so says the Spirit), from here, "Yea, saith the Spirit, that they may rest from their labours; and their works do follow them," (Rev. 14:13). So says the Spirit, not so says the flesh. So much the more spirit a man has so much the more he will say it is blessed, and the more he will pray submittingly for it, quickly. Indeed a godly man, when the flesh is predominate, and the spirit under hatches, then he may be desirous to be spared awhile, O spare me a little, as the spouse may sometimes with her husband, deferring his coming when she is not fit to receive him, the house if not ready, not clean enough.

A crown of righteousness, says the Apostle, *is laid up for all them that love the appearing of the Lord Jesus*, (1 Tim. 4:8). And the second time shall Christ appear to salvation, to all them that look for him, Hebrews 9. Are you then one that looks for Christ, that desires nothing but union with him. He will come to you, for your salvation. If men do not look for him, will he come to them to salvation? It may be in some disease when you can take no pleasure in the world, you wish that you were with Christ. Nature may have a great hand in this.

But in your youth, in the midst of all worldly contents when you are in your pleasant orchard with your wife and children about you, having what your heart can wish, can you say then, now would I most willingly leave all these to go to Christ? When you prefer his company above all things, count that delight the best, that comes from communion with him, then you love the Lord Jesus.

Love is exceeding bountiful, apt to do much for the Lord, and to suffer anything gladly. The Apostle in the first Epistle to the Corinthians, chapter 13, sets down many excellent properties of love. She that loved Christ had a box of ointment. It may be it was the best thing she had. It may be it was all she had, yet she bestows it on Christ. So *Abraham*, when God would have his son, he goes willingly about it, not formally, not out of necessity, but he rose up early to do it. It may be there will come a time when God shall need your wealth, it may be your credit.

Now, you can deny him nothing, if you love him. So *Delilah* would not be persuaded that Sampson loved her so long as he kept back anything from her. If there is anything so near unto you as your life, and it is told to you that the Lord has need of it, he shall have it. You will say, it was a wise action of David to pour out that water as an offering to the Lord which he so longed for, and obtained with the hazard of the lives of three of his worthies. As when a man has a good bit, he will send it to his friend, so in another place, *he would not offer to the Lord of that which should cost him nothing,* (2 Sam 24). But what can I bestow upon the Lord, you will say? If you are a preacher, preach the gospel for Christ. So, every man in his calling, let him do something for the Lord, and if he shall call for your life, let it not be dear to you.

And as love is this bountiful, *so it seeks not its own*, 1 Corinthians 13. And now, how few will be found that love Christ? We may well complain with *Paul*, "All men seek their own and not the things of Jesus Christ," Philemon 2. Paul that loved the Lord, how was he affected? He did not regard himself, did not take care what should become of himself; he took the care of all the churches on him. *Who is offended* and so by taking offense, falls away, *and I burn not*? Are you a minister and love the Lord Jesus, you will not be so careful for a living, and that it is a convenient one, but you would preach as Paul, though for nothing. For every man might do much for the Lord if he sought the things of the Lord; if he did plead with himself, how to bring advantage to Christ.

And then if this should come in, if I do this, I shall hinder my estate, lose my friends, it would be nothing. The love of the Lord would be far better to you than anything. Love does much for the Lord. Faith works by love. He loves much that does much. *Paul*, as he was abundant in love, so in labor. *If you love me*, says our Savior, *keep my commandments*. Are you willing then to take much pains for the Lord? Do you feed the lambs of Christ? If you are a minister, or if you are in the way to that calling, are you diligent to fit yourself for it? And do not love only works, but it makes *the commandments not grievous.* The wife may serve her husband, and the servant him, but with a different affection. The covetous man, when he is before some great man that can imprison him, or put him to death may part with his wealth, or if with one that can greatly prefer him, in hope of that, he may be brought to part with his money. But willingly, he will not. But you must find delight in what you do. When you do a kindness to one that you love, you do but do yourself a kindness on that party. And in this sense, what thanks do you deserve? You do but satisfy your love. As a mother loves her child, and does the offices of kindness to it with delight, though she shall never have anything for it. If you had this love, you would come to say, "Jesus saith unto them, My meat is to do the will of him that sent me, and to finish his work," (John 4:34). Now, you need not be hired to eat and drink.

Lastly, *love suffers all things,* (1 Cor. 13). Are you willing to suffer any thing for the Lord? When David did a religious act, Michal looks on him with another eye, as men look now on religious actions. It is no matter, says *David*, I will bear it, for I did it to the Lord who chose me before your father's house. And if this is to be vile, I will be yet more vile. Can you endure to be pointed at, scoffed and mocked, for the Lord? It was a sore trial to have his wife so against him, yet we see how he did bear it. *Bonds and afflictions,* says *Paul abide me in every city,* but none of these things move me, "neither count I my life dear unto myself, so I may finish my course with joy," (Acts 20:24). Are you able to do this? But I cannot like, you will say to be put to it, you do not know, it may be you may lose your wealth, your credit, and respect among those whom you loved, and this is something. Yet love makes it as nothing. We see when a man loves a maid, neither father nor friend, nor the speech of people will move him to give it over. True, this is a sinful love, but yet shows what the nature of love is. No, I will go further, you will suffer all with joy, *Col 1:11.* So when the Apostles were whipped where the shame was more than the pain, yet they rejoiced that they were thought worthy to suffer for Christ. *Acts 5.*

Put all these together. Are you bountiful that if the Lord should put you to any cost, cost of purse, labors of life, he should willingly have it? Do you take care for the things of Christ, how you may glorify him? Do you do much, and suffer much for the Lord? Take these notes no further than you see reason for them. And know that this is that word of the Lord, if you do not love the Lord Jesus, you are cursed.

The next property of love is, it desires nothing so much as love again. If a man is serviceable to another, and not out of love so he is officious to him, he is content. But love will be paid in its own coin. It will not have mercy without grace. A kingdom without grace will not be contented with it. It is very observant in this kind, *Quis fallere possit amantem?* (*Who can deceive a lover?*) They will be very curious this way. They must see love in everything, or else they cannot take delight in it. It is not a kingdom that can quiet them without the love of God.

However it goes with corn, wine, and oil, their prayer is, *Psalm 4*. If a man's turn was served, so he might be freed from hell, and made happy, and then love him, this man does not love the Lord. That which *Absalom* did in hypocrisy, we are to do in truth, (Sam 14). *What avails it me that I enjoy* (he says) *my lands, and that I live in Jerusalem, so long as I may not see the king's face?* So if God should give you abundance of all your hearts can wish, are you from the fire of hell, yet this will not content you without you seeing his face, if you have this love. And so this to be of God's people, "If my people, which are called by my name, shall humble themselves, and pray, and seek my face, and turn from their wicked ways; then will I hear from heaven, and will forgive their sin, and will heal their land," (2 Chr. 7:14). When a people are oppressed and in captivity, they may come to the Lord and humble themselves, but for their own liberty, they may seek their own good in it, as those in *Hosea 7:14*, but God's people seek his face, his favor. Examine yourself then, if when his countenance is clouded, and he hides his face, you are impatient, you cannot bear it, then you may assure yourself that you love the Lord. So David did in Psalm 51 when he lacked the sense of God's favor, how he complained he would have no denial, and therefore never gives over entreating until he is answered.

Do you love the Lord? Then, you love the saints. This is a true and common note, everyone has it in his mouth, 1 John 3. *If you love the Lord, you will love the brethren.* "We know that we have passed from death unto life, because we love the brethren. He that loveth not his brother abideth in death," (1 John 3:14). Do you then love the Lord, and hate evil in other men? *If you do not love your brother whom you see daily, how can you love the Lord whom you never see?* God is remote from our eyes that we cannot behold him. Now, his image is stamped on the saints, and so is visible to us. We see them daily, they converse with us. Now, if we do not love them, we cannot love God. For, the love of Christ is that holy disposition which you conceive in your mind of him. Now, the same kind is in the saints. As those that do the lusts of the devil, are of his disposition, that is, are as it were little devils. So in the saints, there is the same disposition, the same mind that was in Christ Jesus in the same way.

Objection. But you will say, I would love them, if I thought they were not hypocrites.

Solution. Take heed, you may persecute Christ under the person of a hypocrite. Why do you seemingly think they are hypocrites? Yet a true member of Christ is found wounded by you. And when your heart shall rife against you, out of the side of the likeness of religion and true piety, what would you do if the substance were there, if he had grace in a higher measure? Christ pitches on this note above all others. It is far easier to love a holy man then to love God. For he lives among us. We have him continually before our eyes. Do not say then you love such as are afar off. You do not care for these.

Objection and solution. But you will say I love them well enough, do you so? Do you delight then in their company? Are you in your natural element when you are among them? This you will do by a natural instinct if you love the Lord Jesus. Again, do you hate sin in all? The same ground will cause you to hate sin which moves you to love grace. Do you then hate sin as in dislike, and do you hate sin in regenerate men and their society, no matter if their company is pleasant, so profitable?

Objection. But what, would you have me to hate men then? No, but hate their sin, and love them with the love of piety.

Solution. Let your heart melt to consider their case, and desire their good; love them, but so as it may stand with the love of the Lord Jesus. Look then to yourselves and examine yourselves by these marks. See that you have this love. If you do not have it, you are among the number of these men which are to be *accursed unto death.*

Objection. But, I hope I do not deserve so bad, my nature I hope is not so vile as to not love the Lord Jesus.

Solution. No, you hate him, do you not, hoping

that there was no such Lord to come to judgment, that you might live as you please? Could you with that ever here enjoy these pleasures and never come at him? Now to wish that one were not, what is it, but to hate him? *Quem metuunt oderunt.* We say men hate him whom they stand in fear of. Do you then fear and quake at his coming? Surely then you are haters of God.

Objection and solution. But I hope we are not haters of God. Why, this is not so strange. The Apostle tell us that there were such *as loved their pleasure more than God*, (2 Tim. 3). Yes, and that there were *haters of God also*, Roman 1:30. And in the second commandment God threatens such as *hate him*, (Exod. 20), and you may be one of them. For if you cannot endure his company, if your heart rises against his image, it is plain you are a hater of God.

Objection. What? You would make me out of love with myself. What do you preach damnation to me? If maybe all these signs are not in me. Am I then so accursed?

Solution. Yes, we do preach damnation to all that are in such a case, and we are to threaten the curse. And thus the Lord esteems of you, and it were good that you thought so of yourselves in time. It is the minister's duty to separate the precious from the vile, to distinguish between men, to show you truly what your conditions are. Therefore, apply this text to yourselves, every one. If I do not love the Lord Jesus, I am an accursed men, yes to be had in execration to the death, which might make you loathe yourselves in dust and ashes. It might make sin alive in you, and bring you to love this *Jesus*.

So ends the second sermon.

SERMON 3

1 Cor. 16:22, "If any man love not the Lord Jesus Christ, let him be had in execration, yea let him be accursed unto death."

Now because this love is so needful, we will add more signs for the trial of yourselves, for we cannot be better occupied than to love Christ.

A sixth sign is this, he that loves will be apt to praise and speak well of that which he loves, and he will exceed in it, yes, he is very glad when he hears others speak well of it. So if we did love the Lord, we should be apt to speak well of him, we would be much in the speech of him. When the heart is full of this love of God in Christ, *out of that abundance in your heart, your mouth will speak.* But you speak but little of God, and that little is brought in by company, you are cold in your praising of him. Why do you not love him? See in David, a man that loved the Lord. How much was he in the praising of him? No, he could not be content to do this alone, but he must have *all creatures to praise him and to speak good of his name.* Even as a servant that commends his master invites others to serve him. This love "enlarges the heart and opens the mouth. O Corinthians, our hearts are enlarged towards you, and our mouths are opened," 2 Corinthians 6:11. This is an argument that our hearts are enlarged, that we abound in love when our mouths are opened. So that your heart is straightened towards God, if your mouth is not open to his praises.

Objection. But I cannot speak as other men. I am no scholar, but if I had gifts, learning, I could in this way speak.

Solution. This is no excuse, it is the nature of love to make men eloquent, the passions make eloquent. As we say, *Pectus facit eloquentes, and magna pars eloquentia consira animo.* Are you then apt to speak well of God? But this, you will say, is but a small matter, who does not? O yes, we are lacking in that manner of speaking of him which love requires. We do not speak of him with that affection, that sensibleness, that may inflame others to love him. See the spouse in the *Song of Songs*, O! she says, *my love is fairer than ten thousand.* And so will the soul that loves God do the same. It will tell *of his mercies abroad.* It will *speak good of his name.* And that not as a duty only, but as a thing in which it takes especial delight. Love follows the judgment. You cannot love the Lord, but you will think well of him. See then what your speeches are concerning him. See if your heart nimbly indites, and your tongue be as the pen of a ready scribe. "My heart is inditing a good matter: I speak of the things which I have made touching the king: my tongue is the pen of a ready writer," (Psa. 45:1).

Consider whether you endeavor to do anything for Christ without expostulating, and indenting with him. Whether you are ready to do all things freely to him without consulting with another about it. A friend must not be strict in taking his account, for them he plays the *Huckster*; he does but buy and sell. When you are trying and expostulating then whether such a duty is necessary or not, whether another will not serve the turn, this is a sign you do want love. A minister that has this love, when he is to take a living, will not so much enquire what reward he shall have as what service he may do to God in it. If you did love the Lord, you would not stand saying, is it necessary to keep the Lord 's Day so strictly? You would be ready to do whatever has but a shadow of pleasing him. O! how you would be glad of such a day so free from other busyness wherein you might sequester yourselves from the world, to attend upon God and to enjoy him? So for a family of prayer, you would not ask, can it not be omitted without sin? This questioning will not stand with this love, for the person you serve is the Lord and you must not be as a mercenary servant. A wife will be devising things to please her husband. *So, what shall I render to the Lord* (David says). *So Paul was abundant in labors and sufferings.* If *Paul* would have done nothing but out of necessity, he would have never done half so much, say then, I will even go do my duty, and perform my task. If I must pray in my family, then I will. If I must keep the Lord's Day, I will make a shift to wear out the day. This I say argues a heart void of this love. We must know that Christ has died *to purchase to himself a people zealous of good works.* Such as do good works with desire or dear delight, that would feign do a great deal more than they do. Would you then do no more than just what will bring you to heaven as you think? Do you set limits to your performances? You do not have this love. Why? You pray that you may serve Christ *on earth as the angels do in heaven*, and you, will you say such a man goes less than you do, it is no matter, this pace will bring me to heaven and so never mend it? This is a sign of no love to the Lord Jesus.

If you did love the Lord, you should find a holy affection of anger and zeal rising against such as offend him. Anger waits on love. Love is an affection that makes forwards to the thing beloved, and if anything stands in the way, anger removes it hastily.

If your heart then is not stirred when God is dishonored and his church spoiled, you do not love him. Can you endure to hear yourself scandalized? No, and why? Because you love *yourself*. To see then the blood of the Lord Jesus trampled on, neglected so, as no man should regard it, to see the saints in adversity, and not to be affected, argues that your heart is void of this love of the Lord Jesus.

Eli, when he heard the news of *Israel's* flight, his son's death, it necessarily grieved him, but all this while his heart was composed. But the worst news (as usually it does), comes last. The ark of God was taken. Then his heart was amazed. He could no longer subsist, but he falls down backward and breaks his neck. But it may be that you do not hope to attain to the grace of Eli. Why look then on his daughter-in-law, one of the weaker sex? All that ill news moved her not so much. When the ark of God was taken, that was it which she pitched upon her son that was born and could not allay this grief.

Objection. But the ark is not taken (you will say) there is not the same type of cause now with us.

Solution. No? Are not many churches desolate? When you see so many churches ransacked beyond the seas, do you not see the ark of God taken in a great measure? When you see popery increasing and the saints wallowing in their blood? If you do not take this to heart, it is because the love of Christ is not in you.

If *Christ* loves a man, "It is good neither to eat flesh, nor to drink wine, nor any thing whereby thy brother stumbleth, or is offended, or is made weak. Hast thou faith? have it to thyself before God. Happy is he that condemneth not himself in that thing which he alloweth," (Rom 14:21-22), says the Apostle. When the king, Jer. 36, took that book and burned it, it is noted of those that stood by, *that they did rend their clothes.* God takes it as a great sign of a profane heart, when one shall not take such dishonor of his to hear when he rends not his clothes at the sight of such a thing. *Paul,* when he saw idolatry that abounded in *Athens, was inflamed in his spirit,* (see Acts 17).

See what a commendation God gave to Phineas for his zeal against Zimri and Coshi, he would have it remembered as a special note of his love to him which he would not let go unrewarded. If you do not then pray for the churches welfare, if you are not affected with the loss and disadvantages of the church as with your own, you lack this love.

A ninth sign is not to dare to do anything that displeases him. If you do a thing that would be displeasing, you would rather that all the world should see you, then him whom you love. Now, you know God always beholds you. You should therefore be always alike careful. "They shall fear the Lord and His goodness," (Hosea. 4:2). The Lord for his goodness, they shall fear to lose him. Above all, consider when you have offended him, how you take that to heart. When you know there is a breach between you and the Lord, and you can be content and rest in it, this is a shrewd sign of no love. When man and wife shall fall out, and not grieve for it, but do not let it pass seeking to be reconciled; it is sign of cold love between them.

Think with yourself, there is not a man whom you profess to love, but you would not willingly provoke. And dare you say that you love the Lord, and yet you will grieve and vex him?

If you love the Lord, there would be a hungering

in you after him, there would be still a desire that way. All impediments would be broken though the heart would still be moving towards it. It would be bending there. It would admit no repulse. As the woman of *Canaan*, in Matthew 15, she would not be put off. As the stone does not rest until it comes to the center, so nothing can keep you off from the Lord, no pleasures, away with them, not any difficulties. No, you cannot rest without him.

Do not say then with yourself though you do not love him now, yet I may love him hereafter, and I may love him hereafter though not so much. No, love desires present union. It hates all delays. Consider this, if you did repent out of love, your repentance would be present, and what repentance is it which is not out of love?

Verse 3. To humble ourselves for lack of this love. Then here you are to humble yourself if you are failing in this labor of love. See how great a fault it is, not to love the Lord, and learn to blame yourself exceedingly for it. And that you may do this, I will show you what great reason you have to love the Lord.

1. The reasons we have to love the Lord. Consider that *he is worthy to be beloved.* As *David* said, *he is worthy to be praised.* So may we well say, he is worthy to be *beloved.* And why? Because he has all that is amiable in him. If you see anything lovely in the creature, it is eminently in him. Shall not he that made the eye see? He that made the ear hear? Shall not he that gave these perfections to the creatures have them in himself more eminently?

This perfection of his beauty is that which causes the angels so much to admire and adore him, to be taken up in the admiration of his excellencies. Observe that in any man whom you love there is something *not* to be beloved. But Christ is wholly delectable, there is nothing in him not fully to be beloved. See how the spouse describes him in the *Song of Songs,* how she sets him forth in every part of him most to be desired, if you could but see the Lord. If it did but please him to show himself to you, as he promised to *show himself unto him that loves him,* (John 14:21). If the Lord, I say, would give you a glimpse of himself, if by the light of the Spirit you could see him, you would acknowledge him worthy of your love. And this is the reason that some love him, and others do not, because he discloses himself to some and not to others. As he did to *Moses,* where he let us see a little of his expression of himself. *The Lord, the Lord,* (Exodus 34). This is but the casket, the jewel is within. If God's Spirit should open these words to you, you would see him the fairest of ten thousand, *Jehovah, Jehovah*. Of every creature (you may say) something as it was that it is not, and something is that it will not be. But God is *unchangeable* Jehovah, in him is no alteration, he is not a friend today, and none tomorrow and such a friend you would desire to choose, as this name signifies, his immutable being, so his omnipotency, he is *Almighty*. Now what a loadstone of love is this? All the power in men enables them to bear injurious acts. But the Lord has all abilities, all ornaments, all excellencies, all is comprehended in this *Almighty*. So that well may such a friend be desired.

Objection. True, will the poor soul say he is well worth the having. But he will not match with such a match as I am.

Answer. O yes, he is wonderfully *pitiful and merciful*, as great a Prince of pity as of anything else.

Objection. Merciful, but I have no beauty, no grace in me, no worth, and no repentance.

Answer. But God is *exceedingly gracious*. Kings are said to be gracious because there is supposed such a difference between them and their subjects that they can deserve nothing of them. So *God is gracious.* He does not look for anything deserving in you.

Objection. But I have provoked him by sinning, and sinning often. This will make him put me off.

Answer. No, he is of *great forbearance.*

Objection. But if he does receive me, I must carry myself well, pray and do that which I shall never be able to do.

Answer. Why no, *he is very kind.* Look what a king Father, a kind Husband would do to a child, or a wife. They are careful to give content. The same may you expect of the Lord. He will wink at many infirmities if your desire is found.

Objection. Though he says so, how shall I know *that he will do it?*

Answer. To confirm this, *He is true.* He keeps covenant and has given examples of his mercy on thousands of those that fear him.

Objection. O, but still my sins are many and great.

Answer. Be it so, yet he *forgives iniquities, transgressions and sins,* original sins, sins of weakness and sins of willfulness.

This glory God showed to *Moses*. This is the description of himself. Such a one if Jesus Christ, O you daughters of Jerusalem, and is he not worthy to be beloved?

When you have considered the worth that is in himself, consider that *he sues to you for your love.* Suppose a prince should come and ask this at your hands, would you deny him? The weak should sue to the stronger, but here the Lord God comes to you for your love.

"This is that, O Israel, which he requires of thee, that thou love the Lord thy God," (Deut. 10:16). When such a God shall ask for your love, sue for it, shall he be denied? We (the ministers) are but Christ's spokesmen to woe for Christ. See who it is that requires this? It is your sovereign Lord that might have required you to sacrifice your children, your life, your goods, for his honor and can he not have your love? Now Israel, what does the Lord your God require of you but to fear him, to love him? As if he should say, the Lord has done great things for you and might require great things of you again. This may melt you then, that he requires nothing but your love.

Again consider, he has planted this love in your heart. Shall he not have his own then when he requires?

Shall he not which planted the tree eat of the fruit? Shall he not which gave this fountain of love taste of the waters of it?

Again, on whom would you bestow it, if you will not give it to the Lord? It must be bestowed somewhere and it is the best thing you have to bestow. It sways and commands everything in you. Does your wealth deserve it? Do men deserve it? Why, they are not to be compared to the Lord. Can any man do for you what he does? Besides, he forgives you your sins day by day. Think of his excellencies.

Again, you are engaged to love him. You are married to him. You have given up your names to him in your baptism. So that now I may well call you *an adulterous generation*, if you do not love him, *you are witnesses against yourselves in this day* (Joshua says), (Joshua 24), if you do not serve the Lord. He takes great advantage of their promise that they had made to serve the Lord. You are now witnesses against yourselves if you do not do it.

So all that hear me this day are witnesses against themselves. For in their baptism, they took the Lord for their God. Is he not your master? Where then is your fear? Is he not your Father? Where then is your reverence? Is he not your friend, where then is your love?

Again, he has bought us, yes, he has overbought us. If you should see a flock of sheep and hear that such a man has paid such a price for them, far beyond their worth, you will be ready to say, let him have them. He is well worthy of them. And shall Christ be denied that which he has so dearly bought? He has bought you from the world, from the power of the devil, yes, and from yourselves, so that they are not to set us to work, "What? know ye not that your body is the temple of the Holy Ghost which is in you, which ye have of God, and ye are not your own?" (1 Cor. 6:19). We are therefore to do a mother's business, and that is Christ's who requires love.

Besides all these generalities, think of the particulars which work most on us. See all his passages to you, how kind he has been toward you. See how he has dealt with you from your youth until now. Consider all his kindness bestowed on you. See also what he has done in forgiving you. You have sinned often, and greatly, and yet still he has forgiven you, and this is a great matter. *She loved much because much was forgiven her*, (Luke 7). He feeds you and clothes you. You do not have a night's rest but he gives it you. It is he that keeps you from all dangers, that cares for you when you cannot take care of yourself. The creature cannot help you without the commands to help you. He has stood close to you in all exigents. And this most of all affects us. In some great danger, when all forsake us, we cannot but love him most dearly that sticks close to us. Thus has the Lord done to you. With this *Nathan* urges *David* and aggravates his sin. "The Lord has done this and this to you, and if that had not done enough, would have done more," (2 Sam. 12:8). Take up the same practice with your soul. The Lord has done such and such for me, and shall I not love him? Would we not hate that man that should not love and respect him from whom he has his whole maintenance? (Read Ephesians 3).

Lastly, consider that he loves you. Now as fire begets fire, so love *begets love*. The Son of God has loved and given himself for you. "I am crucified with Christ: nevertheless I live; yet not I, but Christ liveth in me: and the life which I now live in the flesh I live by faith of the Son of God, who loved me, and gave himself for me," (Gal. 2:20). Consider Christ has loved you, and has given a good experiment of his love to you; he gave himself for you. And if he had given you himself whole, it had been a gift inestimable. But he has given you himself broken, *crucified* to you, who has been a rebel against him. See his love, he looks on you when you do not think of him. He took care of you when you took none for yourself. No, then he thought it is not too much to die for your good. O! the height, the length, the breadth, the depth of the love of Christ which passes knowledge. You can never know this love of the Lord, it astonished Paul.

All this may stir you up to fear the Lord. This shows you what reason you have to do it. And it may be an important point to meditate on, or at the least may cause you greatly to condemn yourself for not loving him. Let these at least make you think well of the Lord and ill of yourself, that you cannot love. It will go with you if he is refused. *His wrath will be kindled*, Psalm 2, after he has sued to you and you reject him, he will not put it up, but will make his wrath known on you, which God forbid.

So ends the third Sermon.

SERMON 4

Matt. 22:37-38, "This is the first and great commandment; thou shalt love the Lord thy God with all thy heart."

Psalm 31:26, "Love the Lord O all ye his saints."

1 Cor. 16:22, "If any man love not the Lord Jesus Christ, let him be had in execration, yea let him be accursed unto the death."

4th. Verse – To exhort us to love the Lord. If it is of so much more to love the Lord, that they are accursed that do not love him, let me exhort you then to do it. The motive in the text puts a necessity upon the duty, but to draw you on by the cords of love. See what you shall get by it. It might be a strong argument, you shall perish if you do not do it. But let us see the advantages that will come to us by it.

The advantages which arise from the love of the Lord Jesus. I will make you to keep God's commandments with ease and delight, and this is no small benefit. This love makes you go about the work as the ship with wind and sail. The journey must be gone, now they that do not have love must row and take a great deal more pains. "For this is the love of God, that we keep his commandments: and his commandments are not grievous," (1 John 5:3). This makes us keep the commandments so you may fear, you will say. O, but loves makes them easy. It will be very hard to do them without love. How hard a task would it have been for Paul to have done so much as he did without this love. See what love makes mothers do to their children. *This love of Christ constrained Paul*, it carried him on wings like eagle's. It compelled him to do such and such. And is this then nothing? Yes, it shall make you *abundant in the work of the Lord*. For this commands all the faculties and it winds them up to their highest pegs, and it will make you to do this out of an inward principle. There is a great difference between a horse that runs freely and one that is forced by the spur. Shall not this then cause you to set a high price on this love?

There are scarce any so desperate but they would say they would try to keep God's commandments if they were not so hard. Now this love will make them your delight. It will make them easy and pleasant to you.

This is the surest testimony to your own soul of all others, that *you are translated from death to life.* A hypocrite cannot love the Lord. He may do the outward works. He may hear the Word and be diligent in his calling. But here is the difference, he does not do this out of love. This is that distinguishing character which distinguishes a Christian, as reason does a man. If you can find this love of Christ, this hungering after him, that tendering of the heart towards him, that your heart is to Christ as the iron to the loadstone, you must rest with him. If you can say, I have no great marks of a child of God, I have many infirmities, but yet this I can say, *I love the Lord. My life for yours*, your case is then happy. Heaven and earth may pass away, but you cannot miss of your happiness. Whatever you have, without this can be no sound testimony unto you of your blessedness and this alone may secure you of it.

This love makes you lose nothing, where in the loving of others things, the more you bestow, the less you have. When you give your heart to God, he gives you your heart again, and sets it on work for your own good. "He teacheth us to profit, and leadeth us by the way which we should go," Isaiah 48:17. As Christ said of the Sabbath, the Sabbath was made for man, so may I say of all the commandments, when you give your hearts to the Lord, he sets them to keep the commandments but to this end, that it may be well with you. "O! that there were such a heart in this people to fear me and to keep all my commandments that it might go well with them, and their children forever," (Deut. 5:20). You have your heart again when you give it to God. But here is the difference. Before you were but an unjust professor, now the Lord has made you steward of it, for he has given you leave to love your wives, children, and your lawful recreations, only now you love them at his appointment as he wills, where before you did it as you wished. No, the Lord does not only give you your heart again, but returns it better than it was, new-pointed. As the earth receives in the puddle water which it sends forth clear and pure, all the streams of your love run as fresh for your good as ever they did and more. That only which was amiss in them is taken away. Do not let this feed your understanding only, but find it good in your practice.

By this you shall have much comfort and joy, and this is that which all men desire. What is that which keeps you from loving the Lord? O, you have a conceit that then you must lose your pleasures and your delights. No, it is the most comfortable action in the world to love the Lord. Delights follow action as the flame does the fire. Now the best action has the greatest delight. The philosopher could say, happiness was to love the most amiable object. *Est amare optimum amable,* to love the best amiable known is the best act *whom not seen yet you love, joying with joy unspeakable and glorious.* (1 Peter 1).

It is a pleasant thing to love a creature like yourself, your children, or your friend. But the creature is not perfect and it may be that it does not love you again. But Christ is perfect and loves you, you cannot lose any love by loving Him. O what a pleasant thing it is to love the Lord, to be able to say, *I am my well beloved's and my well beloved is mine.* When you shall consider that the world hates you, what a comfort will it be to know that the Lord loves you, that when the world uses you badly, you may fly to Christ's bosom and lay on him all your grievances. To love and to be beloved, are the most pleasant actions. Now to love the Lord Jesus is so much the more pleasant than the loving of other things, as he is a more excellent object than other things. Besides, is not everything best in its own place, conformed to its own rule, carried to its own end? Take it in your body when all the parts of it are straight, all the faculties and humors in a right temper, serving to their proper ends, then there is delight and comfort. So, love when it is settled on its own objects, sets all things straight, where wonderful joy cannot but follow. *Love has the right things right*, as the schoolman well observes.

Means to love the Lord. Consider this: the love of the Lord makes you a better man, gives you a greater excellency which is a thing which all men desire. Look on the excellency of the creatures, it proceeds from their forms, as the excellency of a pearl above other stones comes from its form. For we know that the matter of all these things is common. Now the object to the faculty, has the property of the form, for it gives name and distinction. Now this love makes God and spiritual things, as it were, the form of the will. And according to this form, is the excellency of the man. Every man is better or worse as his love is pitched on a better object. He that loves a base thing is base, and he that loves a thing something better excels that man, but he that loves spiritual things is the most noble. Look on the lower faculties, when the sensitive appetite enjoys its proper object than a man has his perfection in that kind. So, when the will is fixed on

Jesus Christ, its best object, then a man has his full perfection. If water is united to wind, its made better. When the body is united to the soul, how glorious a creature is it! How glorious a creature then will your soul be when by love it is united to the Lord. This love puts a greater excellency on the soul than the soul does on the body. Love brings the soul to God, and makes him all in all to us so that what we cannot desire we may have in him. Have you not then cause to wish that you loved the Lord? True, you have said enough to inflame us. But how shall we do it my brethren? If you are brought sincerely to desire it, half the work is done. When the disciples prayed, *Lord increase our faith,* Matt 18, Christ answers, *If you have faith but as a grain of a mustard seed, you may say unto this mountain, be you moved and it shall be moved.* But this is not the means to get faith, no, but this *commends* faith. And if out of this commendation they could come to prize and admire it, and so pray earnestly for it, God would give it to them. Let this therefore be the first means to help you to the getting of this, to the *Lord Jesus.*

First, pray heartily for it. Lord, I desire to love you. I see you most amiable, and would feign love you. This petition is according to your will. Lord, grant it to me.

How would this prevail? How could God put off such a request?

Objection. But I have prayed and I have not obtained it.

Solution. But have you prayed importunately as the woman to the unjust judge without giving up? This is a precious grace and therefore God will have us bestow some pains in the getting of it. We shall not obtain it easily so that we may prize it the more, and keep it the more charity. *The grace of Christ,* says Paul, *was abundant with me in faith and love,* (1 Tim. 11:14). This is that which the Apostle magnified so much that God had given him love. The grace of Christ was abundant towards him in giving him love.

Question. But how does prayer do this?

Answer. That little love which moved you to pray, by exercise is increased and is become greater.

Prayer brings you into acquaintance with God. Before acquaintance there may be a wishing well to another, but there cannot be that love to another which is required in friendship.

And it may be that Christ will show himself unto you, as we see when he himself, (*cf.* Matt. 17), *prayed, his garments were changed, and he was transfigured.*

But especially, prayer does this by prevailing with God as we see the prayers of the blind man prevailed with Christ. And do you think that Christ, now in heaven, has put off these kinds of affections which he had on the earth? Will he not also hear if you should pray to him?

Objection. But this you will say is a common means to obtain all grace.

Answer. Yes, but of this love in a special manner, because love is the most peculiar gift of the Holy Spirit. Now the Holy Spirit is obtained by prayer. Our hearts are so carnal, so fleshly, that we cannot love the Lord and he is so holy, so good that we can no more love him unless he himself kindle this flame of love in our hearts than cold water can heat itself unless it had another principle. Contend therefore and strive with the Lord for his Spirit which works this love, who has *declared also unto us your love in the Spirit.* (Col. 1:8).

Secondly, desire the Lord to show you himself, that Jesus Christ would manifest himself unto you. And this is the greatest means of all, to work love. *He that has my commandments, and keeps them, is he that loves me, and he shall be loved of the Father, and I will love him, and show myself unto him,* (John 4:21), when Christ shall show himself to you when he shall open the clouds, and let you see his beauty, his glory. Oh, then you cannot but love him.

There is a great difference between the ministers who sing of you, Christ and his excellencies, and the Holy Spirit. Though we could speak with the tongue of angels, yet it would be but as the dead letter to Christ's showing of himself. When he shall show you your vileness, his excellency, your sinfulness, his holiness, your misery, his mercies, you necessarily love him. *Paul,* when he had revealed Christ, what he could reveal to the Ephesians, he prays for them, that *God would give them the Spirit of wisdom and revelation,* (Eph. 1:18). As who should say, the labor is all lost if you should see no more than I preach. You do not love a man till you know him yourself. The Lord showed himself to Moses, David, Paul, which made them love him so much. Go therefore to the Lord and pray as *Moses, Lord show me your glory,* and beg it earnestly at his hands and that which was done extraordinarily shall be done to your soul. That was but a showing of the Lord by a right light which is done more or less to everyone.

Objection. But this is an act of the Lord. What shall I do to it?

Solution. Consider what the Scripture says of him, what the saints say of him, but most of all what he has been to you. See with what patience, love, and mercy, he has carried himself towards you, as when we converse with a man out of his several actions we gather his disposition, and so frame an idea of him in our mind.

We must humble ourselves, labor to see our miserable conditions, for that will bring love. So Paul, when he considered that he was the worst of all, it made him love more than them all. So Mary, when she conceived how unfit she was to conceive by the Holy Spirit, she sung that song. When we look on ourselves and see our own sins and miseries, our love to Christ will be increased. When a man shall have a true apprehension of himself and his misery, and can expect nothing but death and damnation, and then Christ should come and say *no, but he shall live*, this wounds a man's heart with love. Look on your own secret sins, your relapses, your misery by sin, and then on Christ's coming with his mercies and favors, and you cannot but love him. I say look on your sins, weigh them with their circumstances. Think that, *after so many adulteries* (Jer. 1) committed against Christ, yet that he should say,

If you will come in, yet will I receive you, this might shake you and melt your heart. He that does not love the Lord does not see his misery, nor that good he has by him.

Strengthen your faith, for the stronger your faith is, the greater will your love be. A strong hand rids more work than a weak hand. Take a man excellent in all gifts whom you much admire. Yet, if he did not love you, you would not much care for such a one. So, though you see much excellency in Christ, yet you cannot love him unless you have a persuasion that he loves you. But how shall I know that he will love me? He has made it known that he is yours, and that he is willing to become your familiar friend. God has given him in marriage to you, *to us a child is born, a Son is given.* (Isa. 9) And Christ himself has shown sufficiently his love to you. He has spent his blood for you, yes, he continually speaks to his Father on your behalf, yes he sues to you for love, he loves you first, and sues to you, as the man does to the woman. You may be persuaded therefore that he loves you.

Objection. But I am not fit to be a spouse to Christ.

Answer. It is true, and he knew that well enough. He will take you a blackamoor, and *afterwards will put beauty on thee*, (Ezekiel 36:16). Do not stand on your unfitness when he is your suitor.

But it may be that he stands such and such affected to such and such persons, and how shall I know that the Lord loves *me* and is willing to take *me*?

I can say nothing to you but this, and that is sufficient. You have his general promise made to all, "And he said unto them, Go ye into all the world, and preach the gospel to every creature," (Mark 16:15). There is a general mandate given to ministers to preach the promise to all, and why will you make exceptions where God has made none, and entertain his promises? We are commanded to offer Christ to all, every one that will come may come and drink of this water of life freely. The offer is general, though but some embrace it.

Objection. But I want godly sorrow for my sins. And, this is required before we can receive Christ.

Answer. Yet do not deceive yourself. The matter is not whether your humiliation is more or less, only come. The promise is made to all that come. They shall be refreshed. Indeed you will not come until you are somewhat humbled. You will not fly to the city of refuge till you are pursued by the avenger of blood. But, if you come at all, God will fulfill his promise. Do not stick not so much on the degree of your humiliation. Take a man that has committed high treason for which he is condemned and brought to the place of execution, ready to suffer, but then there is a pardon offered him. And take another guilty of the same crime, but as yet not condemned, and bring him a pardon. He is even as joyful as the other, for he saw his case was even as bad, only it was not so far gone, and he has not lived to long in sorrow. So some men's sins are grosser and their sorrow more violent, other sins are less, but yet such as they see them like to damn them. They therefore are humbled as truly though not so violently. Therefore, though you have not had so much sorrow as others, nor felt those terrors of the Almighty, yet if you have so much as will bring you to Christ and make you stick close to him, so as you would not leave him for anything in the world, it is enough, you shall have him. Why then do you not stick to it? What hinders your faith? The impediments must be on God's part, or on our part. But it is not on God's part, for his promise is full and large, most *free*. Neither is there any on your part, for there is nothing required in you for which he shall set his love on you. There are no merits desired on your part, only accept him, receive him, he will afterwards put some lines on you. Are you willing to take Christ for your husband, for better and worse with a crown of thorns as well as glory? Then the match is concluded. You may be sure that Christ will be yours.

Objection. But I have renewed my sins, and have fallen into divers relapses. I still provoke him and fall back, and God will not endure such a wretch.

Answer. Yet he forgives sins of all sorts. He is *abundant in mercy.* He is still forgiving, and never gives up. There is a *fountain opened to Judah and Jerusalem for sin and for uncleanness,* (Zach. 12:13). There is a fountain, not a cistern, to wash in which may be drawn dry. Only this caveat must be put in, that we do not allow ourselves in any known sin, but that we maintain war continually against sin, and by no means admit any peace with *Amaleck.*

Another means is to remove the impediments of love which are two especially, *strangeness and worldly mindedness.* Strangeness dissolves all friendship. By this means the interest of friendship may be broken off. This strangeness breeds fearfulness when we go to God and fearfulness weakness of love, where boldness is its nurse. *Herein is our love made perfect, that we have boldness in the day of the Lord Jesus.* As by neglecting fellowship with the saints, we come to lose our acquaintance we had towards them, so the neglecting of maintaining our acquaintance with God brings us quite at last to leave him. Draw near, therefore, to God continually, and this will increase your love to him. Therefore, be often in speaking to him and hearing him speak to you.

Be much in prayer, and often in reading and hearing. And do not do these things customarily, and untowardly, but with life and affection. Go to prayer as you would go to speak with your most dear friend whom you most of all delight to talk with. Let it be pleasant to you to converse with him in all things when you have any injury befallen you. Go and make your cause known to him, and when any sin has escaped you, by which he may be offended, do not give over until reconciliation is made, and your friendship solidified. Look especially to your ways, for sin alienates and restrains a man from God, therefore see that it may be removed as much as may be.

Worldly mindedness also hinders the love of God. This is the uncircumcision of the heart. Here it is that the Lord your God will *circumcise your heart, and the heart of your seed to love the Lord your God with all your heart*, *that you may live.* And until the heart is circumcised, it is filled with the love of the world, so that he cannot love the Lord, at least, with all his heart as he ought.

There is no such quenching to the love of God, as the love of the world. Pleasures and the love of carnal things are very apt to steal away our hearts from God before we are aware. If we do not look more narrowly to it, they may do it. Examine your own hearts, and see if by it how much the more you love the world, by so much the less you are affected to the Lord. These things, as *Absalom*, steal away our hearts from God, as he did the people from his Father. If you do not find that love to God which formerly has been, see what has come between God and your heart. Look and see if some pleasure or lust has not crept in between, for these will separate between God and you. See if there is not in your understanding conceits of things to be better than indeed they are, for these will turn the heart from the Lord, but above all, look to your will and affections.

So ends sermon 4.

SERMON 5

Matt. 22:37-38, "This is the first and great commandment, thou shalt love the Lord thy God with all thy heart."

Psalm 31:26, "Love the Lord O all ye his saints."

1 Cor. 16:22, "If any man love not the Lord Jesus Christ, let him be had in execration, yea let him be accursed unto the death."

Now the next thing we have to do is to show *what kind* of love the Lord accepts, for he will not take *any* kind of love that is offered him, but only such a love as he calls for, as he requires.

You must love him with all your might and with all your strength. A public person may do more than a private. His example may do much or he may command others, if not to do good, yet to refrain from evil.

God desires that you love him with all your strength, if you *know* much, you must *do* much. Besides some things you cannot do, namely, which others cannot do without great difficulty. As some men are temperate, some patient by nature. If you are such a one, God requires more of you than of another, for he accounts that which you cannot do without setting your might to it as nothing. It is not enough for you to love the Lord, but you must love him with your might. The might of a rich man, of a magistrate, of a scholar, or whatsoever you are, when you shall come to the Lord with a small pittance, when you have opportunity to do a great deal more, the Lord will not take it at your hands. As a landlord will not receive a small parcel when the tenant may pay a greater sum, neither is this a thing indifferent for you to do, or not to do. For *God requires much of him to whom he has given much.* He gives us all talents which he puts as prizes in our hands which he expects we should lay out according to as we have received. Paul did not work of supererogation though he was *abundant in the works of the Lord,* continually setting himself about the work with his whole strength.

You must love him above all things, else, above all creatures, above that which is most dear unto you, yes, above yourself. And if you do not, you love him but as a creature which will not serve his turn. He has done more for you than any creature has or can do. He has died for you, has given himself crucified for you. He deserves therefore more love than your pleasures, profits, or than any friend you have. You are therefore to love him above all, to embrace and cleave to him chiefly, to make him wholly yours.

Objection. But how can he (you will say) be wholly mine seeing so many have their parts in him?

Answer. Yes, he is wholly yours, and you must be wholly his. He is infinite and so has no parts, but is entire to everyone as every line drawn to the center may challenge the whole center for its own, though there is a thousand lines beside.

Objection. But what? Must I so love the Lord that I may not love earthly things?

Answer. Yes, you may love them so that it is not with an *adulterous* love. You may love them for good, as by them you may be enabled to serve God the better.

Objection. But how shall I know this adulterous love?

Answer. When you love anything so as it lessens your love to your husband, that is an adulterous love. As when those love some pleasure and delight so, as it takes up the mind and hinders you in hearing, and will not suffer you to pray without distraction, but your thoughts must be on it, this love is adulterous love. You may rejoice yet so as if you rejoice not. As this joy does not hinder your walking with God, so you may labor in your calling with a love to it, yet so as it does not draw away your heart from God.

Objection. But this is very difficult (some will say).

Answer. No, it is easy. When God has put this love into your heart, the necessity of it may make it easy. You may do it, or you cannot be saved. Indeed, it is impossible for a man that has set his heart on riches to remove it off again of himself. And in this sense, Christ speaks when he says, "It is so hard for a rich man to enter into the kingdom of heaven." But when God has worked this love in you and has revealed to you the emptiness and vanity of other things, it will be easy.

Objection. But I am not able to love the Lord above myself and all other things.

Answer. Yes, you may if once you are thoroughly persuaded that he is your chiefest good, and how miserable you are without him. You will then be content to forsake and to cleave to him alone.

A man that sows corn is content that it should die, so as it may be quickened again and bring forth more. And therefore Paul, though he saw the outward building of his body go to decay, he did not care, so long as he *was renewed in the inner man.* "That he would grant you, according to the riches of his glory, to be strengthened with might by his Spirit in the inner man; That Christ may dwell in your hearts by faith; that ye, being rooted and grounded in love," (Eph. 3:16-17). So when you see your good contained in him more than in yourself, when you see your happiness laid up in him, you will easily be persuaded to leave yourself to enjoy him. For you lose nothing by losing yourself, your whole happiness is in God.

Again, you must be *rooted and grounded in love.* This is that which the Apostle so prays for the Ephesians, *cf. Ephesians 3:17.* There is a certain love by which God does not accept. When men come and offer to God great promises like the waves of the sea, as big as mountains, O they think they will do much for God. But their minds change and they become as those high waves which at last fall level with the other waters. If a man should proffer you great kindnesses, and you should afterwards come to him to make use of him, and he should look strangely on you as if he were never acquainted with you, how would you esteem of such love! If we are now on, now off in our love, God will not esteem of such love, and if you are not rooted in your love, you will be unstable. Let then your love be well-rooted. Let the foundation be good on which it stands. Now that point is on two things.

1. *In which grounded love does stand.* This love must be *founded in faith.* Therefore, Ephesians 3 when the Apostle had prayed that they might be strengthened in faith, he adds this also, that they *might be grounded in love.* When you are once rooted in faith, you shall be grounded in love. When therefore you come to believe and consider whether Jesus Christ belongs to you, or no, do it not overly and slightly, but do it thoroughly. Sift everything to the *minutia,* do not give anything over until you are fully satisfied, until you can answer all objections, and rest in this persuasion, that all is most true which has been revealed to you of the Lord Jesus Christ, and it is good for you to rest on it.

Your love must be built on his person. If you love his gifts, and not him, you will be unstable in your love. If you love him in his *person,* you do not change, for your love will be constant. But if you love him for what he has done for you because he has done you much good and give you many favors, and tokens of his love, and kept you from many troubles, when he changes his dealing towards you, you will change your love to him. You will then do as Job, receive good from the hand of the Lord and also evil. But in case God should take from you and send one affliction in the neck of another, this will try your love, whether in this case you will stick close to him. Sometimes God hides his face from his children and *writes bitter things against them*. If then you can love him , your love is on his person, a constant love.

Another condition of our love is that is *must be diligent*. The Apostle commends the Thessalonians *effectual faith and diligent love*, (1 Thessalonians 1:3). If you say you love the Lord, and yet will do nothing for him, you do not have that love which God accepts. This love is operative, diligent, and not idle and dead. We do not regard a dead drug, a dead plant. We cut it up and cast it away. Even so does the Lord esteem of a dead love, and love that does not shows its life, its diligence to obey God. This love will cause you to put on new apparel, to adorn your life so as your love may take delight in you. This will make you careful to beautify yourself with the graces of the Spirit. See therefore whether your love prepares you for Christ. This love does that which *John the Baptist* did. It prepares men for the receiving of the Lord. If you will come then before him in your old garments, it is a sign that you do not love him. Again, the operativeness of it is seen in opening your heart to him when he offers himself to you. This will give you a capable heart to entertain him that he may dwell plentifully in you. This does make you *comprehend with all the saints what is the height, and breadth, and length, and depth of the love of Christ*, (Ephesians 3). This love is diligent in cleansing the heart, that it will suffer nothing to remain there that may be offensive to the Lord God that dwells with his people. This love therefore will suffer no sin to remain in the heart, but keeps all clean. It cleanses a man from *all filthiness of flesh and spirit*, (2 Corinthians 5).

Lastly, the diligence of love is seen in the keeping of his commandments. If you do nothing for the Lord, you do not love him. So much love as those have, so much care will there be in you to do his will, so much fire, so much heat to stir for his glory. So much love, so much desire to walk in perfect obedience before him.

The object on whom our love must be set. And now we come to the object on whom our love must be placed, the *Lord Jesus.* Consider whom it is, whom, if you do not love, I pronounce you *accursed.* It is the Lord Jesus, he is your Lord, your Prince, your Savior, your Messiah, your Prophet, so that he which does not love him is worthy to be accursed.

First, he is *our Lord.* Now, to run from an ordinary master is punishable, to rebel against an ordinary king deserves death, but he is more our Lord and King in a more special bond. Besides that, he has made us and preserves us, we are his by purchase and he has bought us dearly, he has shed his blood for us. So that, he that will not love this Lord, let him be accursed.

Secondly, again he is our Savior and in this respect, love is now more due to God then in the time of innocence. When *Adam* broke the covenant and made shipwreck, Christ offered himself as Savior. Now if we will not receive him, there is no more hope. He is the *secunda sabula, the second sand,* left to us after shipwreck, which if we let go, we cannot escape eternal destruction.

Lastly, he is our Prophet, *that Messiah,* John 4, which reveals to us all things. That great Prophet which Moses foretold, which if we do not believe, we are *accursed.* The time of our darkness God did not regard, but now he will have us know now that the light has shone on us, and he has revealed himself when this foretold Prophet has come to us. He has shown himself to us. Now God chains our love, and if now we are not chained to love him, and to come in to him, we are rebels. Yes, he is our *Priest* and would reconcile God and us to him. Yes, he is made to us a *King,* to subdue our lusts and rebellious affections, to draw us to himself, as it were by force. So that now if we do not love him, we *deserve* the curse. Now mark this point that the Lord has joined these two together, the *Lord Jesus.* We must take heed that we do not separate them. He is both *Lord* and *Jesus; sovereign* and *anointed.* And we must see that we do not take him only as a Savior, but also as a Lord. He is not only the author of the remission of our sins, but he is our Lord to rule us. The preaching of the gospel is nothing but the offering of Christ, his whole person, and so you must take him as a subject to be your Lord, as a spouse to be ruled and guided by him, and then we shall have the benefit which arises. We are willing to part with the sweet, but we will have none of the sour. As that rich young man would have had Christ, but he would not part with his wealth for him. But Christ tells him that he must either part with him or them. Can you be content to fare as I do? To be rejected and scorned in the world as I am? Then well good, you may follow me, but otherwise you cannot. And if you are content to do this, to suffer persecution, and to forgo all for him, you shall have him, and all the benefits that come by him. If not, you are not worthy of him. He that does not believe the Lord Jesus is condemned already, *i.e.*, he that does not take him when he is offered is in the state of condemnation. We must see therefore that we take his whole person, as he is a Lord as well as he is a *Savior*, and not the latter without the former. *If any man does not love the Lord Jesus, let him be hid in execration, yes let him be accursed to the death.*

Of the curse of those that do not love the Lord Jesus. The Apostle curses such as do not love him with a double curse. He expresses it in two languages. They are men set apart to evil, appointed to destruction, as some men are set apart to good, so are these to evil. They are shut up in prison, such as God has set himself against. His eyes are continually on them for evil. So shall he be accursed that does not love the Lord Jesus. There shall be a curse on his soul for the matter of grace, that as Christ cursed the fig tree when he came and found no fruit on it, *never fruit grow more on you, and it withered away.* So when Christ is offered and this gospel preached, and you refuse this grace, you may find Christ to curse you, that you will be ever barren in the matter of grace. And if perhaps you think this is no great matter, the curse goes further. You shall be cursed from the *presence of the Lord.* You shall have no part nor portion in his light, sweetness and comfort of his favor. And this *Cain* took to heart, though he was a wicked man, and had before but God's common favor, and so Saul was exceedingly cast down when as God would not answer him by any of those usual means, but is this such a horrible thing to be excluded from his presence. Yes, and at the time of death you shall find it something, yes, in troubles you shall see it a dreadful thing (as they did) to want him to stand as your friend. As Saul did, though in his prosperity he regarded it little, yet when the Philistines came on him, he was driven to his wits end because the Lord would not answer him. But these are but spiritual things. I do not feel them, you will say. But yet the curse goes further, *You shall be cursed also from the earth,* that is, from earthly comforts which it yields to others. Now you shall bestow all your travail and pain on it, and be never the better for it.

Objection. But many a man does not receive him, and yet is not so accursed.

Answer. Indeed, we do not see it many times, and it may be the time of execution is not yet come. You may have *Cain's* privilege, though you are accursed, that none shall kill you presently. You may enjoy your health and wealth, and no man lay hold on you here to hurt you. But you are reserved to a more solemn day of punishment. And yet, the curse goes a step further. *You shall be cursed eternally.* But that, you will say, is a great way off, and you need not fear it yet. But consider what eternity is, what those days of darkness will be when the Son of comfort shall set, and never rise again on you; when it shall be always perfect night, and never day. When God shall open all the treasures of his wrath and power them with full fury on you. When the storm of vengeance shall never be blown over, but you shall be overwhelmed in the midst of all misery as the old world was in the deluge.

If this is the case of men that refuse, yes, that do not love the Lord, then take heed to yourselves. We, the ministers, offer you Christ when we preach and you sit negligently before us, minding other things, not caring to take the Lord. Take heed: this is your portion to be so accursed.

The gospel has two parts. If you take Christ,

you shall be happy, and you shall be saved. But if you will not love him and embrace him, you shall be damned. Therefore, do not think that there is nothing but honey in it, yes there is a sting that follows it if it is neglected. Ministers are not to go a begging in the offering the gospel, but are as ambassadors of the Lord of Heaven. If men will receive our message, so it is, otherwise the dust which we shake off from our feet shall be a witness against you, so that God will shake you off. God will not have his gospel refused, his son despised, and therefore he counsels us, "to kiss the Son, lest he be angry and we perish all in his wrath," (Psalm 2). Though he is a Lamb and behaves meekly among us, yet if we provoke him, we shall know that he can show himself as a Lion. If he is not entertained in the full voice, he will come in fire, in a wind that shall rend the rocks asunder. So he describes himself, "One that hath feet like burning brass, out of whose mouth proceeds a fiery sword," (Revelation 1). *Moses* went first to Mount Gerizim to bless the people, and if that would not move them, he goes up to *Mount Ebal*, and then curses them. So the Apostle before exhorts and persuades them to the love of Christ, but if they will not embrace him on fair terms, he tells them what shall follow. They *must* be *accursed.*

Objection. But what if I do not take the Lord at this instant? I hope this curse will not befall me.

Answer. It is true we cannot say so, for while this time lasts, we are still commanded to offer Christ. Yet, there will come a time when there will come forth a decree which shall never be revoked. Take heed therefore for this is very dangerous. The Lord will not suffer his gospel to be abused or neglected when once the husbandmen refused the Son. They were presently cast out of the vineyard, Matt. 21. This offends God more than any sin that we can commit. To refuse Christ offered is worse than drunkenness, theft, adultery, or the like, which men count the grossest sins. *My people would have none of me, therefore I gave them up to their own hearts lusts.* This refusing him made him swear that they should never enter into his rest. As the gospel offers great favor than the Law, so *swifter damnation* attends the neglect of it. My brethren, take heed that *you receive not the grace of God in vain.* While it is called today, *harden not your hearts,* yes, take heed of refusing it now. For you do not know whether this offer may ever be made to you again, and if it is, you do not know whether you shall have the grace to receive it, or not. Know that the same gospel is a *savor of life unto life*, to such as receive it, but unto the others, *a savor of death unto everlasting death.*

But the gospel is *continued still.*

It is true, but how many are there that live in the congregation, and are never a bit better though they hear the Word daily because by the contempt of it, it becomes the favor of death to them, and their hearts are hardened, so that they shall never receive good by it!

FINIS

A SOLILOQUY

Good *reader*, if you will see the riches of a devout soul after this love of Christ, expressed in these pious sermons, read this soliloquy following.

A Soliloquy of a devout soul to Christ,
panting after the love of the Lord Jesus.

You love of all loves, you chiefest of ten thousand, you loved me before I was. You do love me when I am existing. You do love me (if I am yours) when I am here no more. *Your loves are better than mine,* but mine are worse the gall and wormwood. You love me who deserve less than nothing. I do not love you who deserve more than all things. I have hid myself from you as *Adam,* yet you have opened yourself in the face of my soul, yet in the sight of this sun I have not loved you *pierced through the dark cloud but you loved me.* No baseness of mine has closed your eyes, and kept your heart from me, yet, every base pleasure and pleasing lust has kept my heart and eye from you. Without my love to you, I cannot have my happiness *applied and enjoyed.* It is faith that marries you to me, but this faith must *work by love,* or my marriage will end in a fruitless barrenness, and faithless separation. Here, therefore, I have loved you, but *for lust,* not *for love.* I would have you save me, but I would not honor and please you, I can so think of my disloyalty towards you, but you knew it before I thought it, and more than I can speak or think. You do *think thoughts of love and peace to me,* but I mind the abuse of your love, and the too late repentance of *you on my own terms.* How can I be acceptable to you, *my love, my dove, my undefiled.* You spread out your hands, and are ready for blessing me, but if I open my head, heart, hand, I am apt to receive nothing but *anathema, maranatha* from you. Can love come to enmity, heaven to hell? I am hell (*my Lord*), you are heaven. I am hatred, you are love. You *show hatred,* yet in my *wisdom am I very enmity.* Can I then expect either to have the *blessing* of love, or to avoid the curse of not loving? Show me your face for it is comely. You have often showed me your riches, and I have loved them, but O! show me yourself that I may love you. I have seen your goodness, mercy, compassion, redemption, salvation, and have cried out (*my blessed Jesus*) make these mine. Now let me see yourself that you may be *my beloved and my beloved may be mine*, and all those riches in you. From the sight of your riches, I have desired to preserve myself, from seeing yourself I shall desire to draw near to you, and to cleave to you forever. O you whom my soul desires to love, *show me then where you lie at noon*, that I may see you. I know where I shall find you at the right of my life. I shall find you sitting on yonder throne, ready to say, either, *come ye blessed*, or *go you cursed*. I do not know whether so short a view shall bring me to hear either the one, or the other. Show me then where you lie *at this my noon*. Now your Sun shines on this my tabernacle, and I have some time to behold your beauty, that I may be in love with your person, where then shall I find you? If I look to *Mount Tabor*, I see you in glory, and I cannot but love you for that. If I look *to the garden*, I see you lying on the cold ground, sweating *drops of blood* for me, and I cannot but love you for that. If I look to Golgotha, I see you nailed *to the cross*, and your heart broached, that I may drink your blood and live, and I cannot but love you for that. If I look to *Mount Olivet*, I see you ascending *far above all heavens*, and I cannot but love you for that also, Indeed in *Tabor* you had visible glory, but it soon vanished. In the *garden and Golgotha*, you had little visible *beauty why I should desire you*, and in *Olivet*, you were quite carried out of my sight. If then you lie for me nowhere else, what hope have I to love you, O you to be beloved of all. Are you not in the tents of the shepherds? Do you not walk *in the midst of the golden candlesticks*? Do you not dwell in the hearts of men by faith? O let me see you here below in the church, in myself. Let your glory go before me that I may love you forever, and ever, and be blessed in you. You have a long time been manifested to me in your natures, offices, and marks for me, and these draw me to love you. You have been crucified before my eyes, and the virtues of it have been cleared by the ministry of the Word, and Sacraments. I have heard and seen the *promises, signs, and seals* of your dearest love, and these might allure me to love you. But (*O you Chiefest of ten thousand*) why have you kept yourself at such a distance? Why have you not been *formed in me*? Why have you not dwelt in me, that I might see in you the glories, and virtues, of your life, death, resurrection, ascension, and to be *sick of love*? You have *stood and knocked* at the door of my unworthy heart for this end. You would have *come in and supped with me* after the noon-shine of the gospel with your own banquet. But, alas, there was no room for you because I desired first to feast it out with the base guests of sinful lusts before I would give you entertainment. The cause has been in myself that I have not been better acquainted with you, and so, that I do not have love for you. O wretched soul that I am, *who shall deliver me* from being an enemy to myself! I have *bowed my knees to the Father of you*, the Lord Jesus, that he would grant to me according to the riches of his glory, that I may have his assistance to empty myself of all my wicked guests that you may come into me, and I may have the better list and leisure to contemplate your glory, and be grounded in your love, O my blessed *Lord Jesus*. If I could but get this my gains would be unspeakable. Whatsoever you *command would be sweet* because I love you. If I could give you my heart, you would give it better to me again, for no unclean thing can come out of your hands. But (O my desired love), I have denied you, therefore, I deny myself. I have rejected you, therefore, I reject myself. Do with me as you will, only first love me, and let me answer you with love again. And why should I not be confident to be heard in this, seeing you (*my love*) *sit at the right hand of God making requests for me.* Speak you the word, and your poor servant shall love you. Say to my soul, *My Father has heard your prayer*, and then, *I will love you dearly, my Lord Jesus*, if I love you, I live. If I do not love you, I perish under a fearful curse for evermore. And shall it be so with me, *O you that will not the death of poor sinners*, who pant after you? No, no, your mercies and intercession have prevailed with my God. I find the filth of domineering sin in some measure, washed from the windows of my soul, that the beams of your glory may pierce it, and draw my love after you. Now do I begin to be *sick of love*, and earnestly desire your company here, *by grace*, and hereafter by *glory*. I love to hear you speak (*let me hear your voice for it is sweet*), and to speak to others of you and your beauties. You have made me something willing to do, and to suffer anything for you, *Lord perfect this good work*. If I see the meanest persons, unlike you in your goodness, *my delight is in them*. I love them the better for your sake. I do not dare to willfully anger you, and *my soul is vexed* with them that do it. Thus the pulses of my soul (by your blessing) do begin to beat after you. But (alas) when I consider how weak I am in you love to you my *Savior*, when I find a thousand things creep in between you and home, they steal my heart away from you. When I feel how easily I am diverted from you and your service, what comfort can my poor soul have now?

O my Lord Jesus, you will not leave your own work and suffer your *tender plant to wither away!* When you have sowed your seed, have you not prepared the former and latter rain? *Shall I not be able to do this through him that loves you and me?* I may not run from your love, *you are my Lord.* I dare not, *you are my Jesus.* If you live, let me know your love to me. If I live, let me feel my love to you. *O shed it more in my heart*, that as in believing in you *my person* is justified, so in loving you my faith may be justified, and in having *faith working by love*, I may so constantly walk in your presence, that with comfort I may sing with the Bride, *come Lord Jesus, come quickly.* Even so, *Amen.*

FINIS

www.ingramcontent.com/pod-product-compliance
Lightning Source LLC
Chambersburg PA
CBHW022154080426
42734CB00006B/435